BRITISH MINING

FRONGOCH
LEAD & ZINC MINE

by

David Bick
with contributions by A.J. Parkinson,
Dr C.S. Briggs and Roy Fellows

A
MONOGRAPH
OF THE
NORTHERN MINE RESEARCH SOCIETY
JULY 1996

Tramlines, slag heaps and pieces of machinery,
That was, and still is, my ideal scenery.
(W.H. Auden)

NOTE It should be emphasised that old mines are potentially dangerous, especially underground, and that private land should not be entered without permission.

ISSN 0308 2199

ISBN 0 901450 47 2

Typeset in 10 point Times New Roman

PRINTED

by

RYTON TYPING SERVICE

29 Ryton Street, Worksop,

Notts.

for the publishers

THE NORTHERN MINE RESEARCH SOCIETY

KEIGHLEY U.K.

Cover Illustration:
Frongoch about 1900, showing the towering headframe at Vaughan's New Shaft.
(G.J. Williams).

CONTENTS

PLATES

NOTES AND REFERENCES.

Recurring references are indicated as follows:

B.G.S.	British Geological Survey, Aberystwyth.
Bick	Bick, David *The Old Metal Mines of Mid-Wales*, parts 1-6 (Newent: The Pound House, 1993).
Crosswood	Crosswood Deeds & Documents, National Library of Wales.
Jones	Jones, O.T. *Special Reports on the Mineral Resources of Great Britain Vol.20 Lead & Zinc: The Mining District of North Cardiganshire and West Montgomeryshire* (Sheffield: Mining Facsimiles, 1986. Reprint of 1922 Edition).
Jones MSS	O.T. Jones papers, NLW.
Lewis	Lewis, W.J. *Lead Mining in Wales* (Cardiff: University of Wales Press, 1967).
M.J.	*Mining Journal*.
M.W.	*Mining World*.
N.L.W.	National Library of Wales, Aberystwyth.
P.R.O.	Public Record Office, Kew.

FRONTISPIECE: John Taylor in 1825. Portrait by Sir Thomas Lawrence for the Athenaeum Club.

PREFACE TO FIRST EDITION (1986)

This monograph had its origins in 1982, when the Welsh Mines Society drew the attention of the Royal Commission on the Ancient and Historical Monuments of Wales to the three Cornish Enginehouses and other structures at Frongoch.

The Commission responded with a detailed survey of this unique group of 19th century mine-buildings, and has also generously contributed towards the cost of publication.

Having known Frongoch for almost forty years, I have derived no little pleasure in compiling an historical account. An Appendix by Dr Stephen Briggs (Trefenter) has also been included, based on Moissenet's visit in 1860.

Though nature and man have dealt harshly with the remaining structures, enough still stands to form a basis for a first-class interpretative centre for the history of lead mining in the Principality, as well as a valuable area of general amenity. It is hoped that something can be done in this direction before decay renders the task insuperable.

I should like to take this opportunity to express grateful thanks to Professor D.G. Tucker and Mr Peter Smith, without whose interest in the furtherance of studies relating to Industrial Archaeology, this publication would not have come to pass.

My old friend George Hall has again assisted with references in the *Mining Journal*, and I have to thank him for introducing me to Pontrhydygroes, home of the Lisburne Mines, in 1947. I am also indebted for help in various ways to Douglas Hague, Richard Bird, Simon Timberlake, Jeremy Wilkinson, R. Alan Williams, Simon Hughes, A.J. Parkinson, Dr C.S. Briggs and the staff of the British Geological Survey and the National Library of Wales.

AUTHOR'S NOTE TO NEW EDITION

I am grateful to the NMRS for publishing this enlarged edition, and to Hazel Martell, Mike Gill, Roy Fellows, Mike Moore and Rob Southwick for help in various ways. The demand for the original book has illustrated the potential for further collaboration, and thanks are again due to the Royal Commission for financial aid.

As for the site itself, Scheduled Monument status has done nothing to arrest a continuing decay into hopeless ruin and, with it, all those aspirations expressed above. On the other hand, bearing in mind how integrity elsewhere has suffered in the name of amenity and conservation, perhaps it is better that things remain as they are. If there is an answer, we have have not found it yet.

David Bick, FSA, Pound House, Newent, Glos.   November 1995

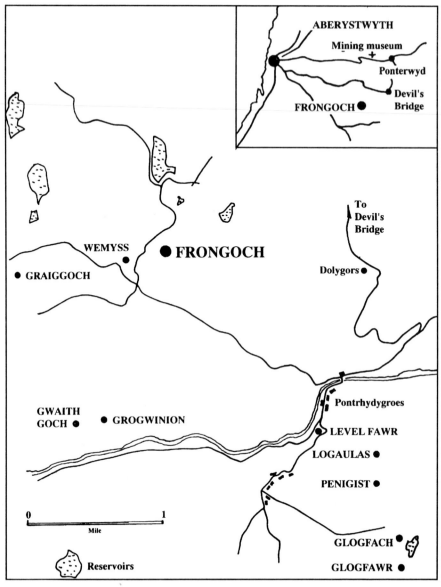

FIG.1 Location map.

INTRODUCTION

Situated in an isolated upland area 11 miles east of Aberystwyth, Frongoch was one of a hundred mines in a county famed for its lead and silver.[1] Of relatively recent origins, it could claim neither the antiquity of workings such as Cwmystwyth, visited by Leland, nor the renown of the silver-lead mines of Goginan and Cwmsymlog which brought great wealth to their promoters in the 17th Century. Nevertheless, with a combined output of well over 100,000 tons of lead ore (galena) and zinc ore (blende), Frongoch was easily the most productive mine in Cardiganshire, and much the biggest producer of blende. However, the latter mineral was very much the poor relation, fetching substantially lower prices than galena.

Frongoch and other mines near Pontrhydygroes belonged to the Vaughans of Crosswood (the Earls of Lisburne), but around 1790 came under the influence of Lord Powys, presumably by an agreement which endured for a number of years. The Powys family had earlier made, and dispersed, a fortune from another lead mine, at Llangynog, and were ever anxious to turn to account other likely prospects.[2]

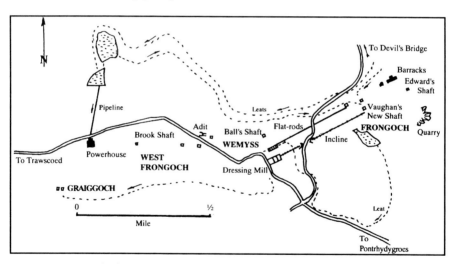

FIG.2 A general plan of Frongoch, Wemyss, West Frongoch and Graiggoch (Red Rock), based on the 1904 sale catalogue.

An influential promoter was John Probert of Shrewsbury, who in 1778 was the Powys agent or manager. He opened mines on his own behalf as well as those of his master, and at times it is difficult to know where his allegiance lay. By 1790 almost every mine of importance south of the Rheidol was in his hands. And, notwithstanding low ore prices because of the French Revolutionary Wars' interfering with export trade, he took up Frongoch.[3] It was then only a small affair, sometimes called Brongoch, and another slight working just to the east was also developed.

For the benefit of the industry, Probert set up a lead-smelting works at Aberystwyth, but, because of a variety of unfortunate circumstances, it proved uneconomic and closed in 1791. Thenceforth ores were shipped either to South Wales, Deeside or Bristol.[4]

The Manager of Probert's mines in Wales was James Lowe, who lived at Dol-y-gors (SN744740), on the road from Devil's Bridge to Pontrhydygroes. He died in the winter of 1793/4 and his son John took over for a while, before being replaced by another outstanding man in mid-Wales, Job Sheldon. He also operated mines of his own, including Cwmsymlog, and in 1808 became partner with Probert. Sheldon proved an astute businessman and eventually made a considerable fortune. He was Mayor of Aberystwyth thirteen times and died in 1844 aged 84.[5]

The principle of common management continued and, from 1824, all Lord Lisburne's mines were leased directly to Williams of Scorrier, a well-known Cornish firm of mine promoters. But times were not propitious. Almost immediately lead began to fall in price, and by 1834 had sunk to less than half its value of 1825, ruining all hope of profit. The Williamses lost well over £20,000 and in 1833 surrendered every lease excepting the silver mine of Llanfair Clydogau.

Fortunes now changed, and the next party, John Taylor & Sons, benefitted from a much improved market that endured for 40 years. Under their control the Lisburne mines rose to a pre-eminent position, with Frongoch the biggest producer. In all, dividends of nearly a quarter of a million pounds were paid on an outlay of only £7,500.

Before the industry became sufficiently established to sustain local foundries and engineering works, such as Greens of Aberystwyth and Mills of Llanidloes, machinery had to be shipped by coaster and dragged by horses over roads that scarcely existed. Transport costs always proved a heavy burden, and the present road from Pontrhydygroes down the Ystwyth valley is a legacy of the Taylors' investment to improve communications. The Manchester and Milford Railway, projected in 1860 on a route that would have taken it past the doorstep of the Lisburne Mines, unfortunately never came to fruition.

Waterwheels were the traditional source of power for the industry, but Frongoch was poorly situated in this respect, with more than usual interruptions from frost and drought. As we shall see, steam was tried, but only served to underline the indispensibility of the older method. Steam, which had done so much for Cornwall, influenced the destiny of mining in mid-Wales hardly at all.

By the late 1870s Frongoch was past its best and, with lead prices falling, the Taylors pulled out. A new company, under John Kitto of Llanidloes, continued in hopes of better days, but the market never recovered. That the mine was able to continue for over 20 years was mainly due to huge reserves of blende which the Taylors had left standing in the workings. In 1881 Frongoch gave employment to over 300 men, women and children – a number only slightly exceeded in the whole of mid-Wales by Van mine near Llanidloes.

The high running costs of an old mine over 900ft deep did not deter a Belgian company from making a very large investment in 1898, however, by installing modern hydro-electric and steam generating plant for all-electric operation. The reasons for this foreign interest are unclear, but within a year or two the evidence of a disastrous commercial blunder was plain. In 1904 the almost new equipment was auctioned at a fraction of its cost. With little or no prospect of work in the neighbourhood, many miners emigrated or went into coal mining - a job which, although less unhealthy, was always considered as practically beneath contempt.

Since then mining at Frongoch has ceased, notwithstanding various proposals for a revival. The huge dumps were largely removed for treatment in the 1920s. The site is now a waste-land, increasingly encroached upon by a sawmill, with the shells of huge Cornish engine-houses and other buildings standing in mute testimony not only to a great mine, but also to a Welsh industry that endured on and off for 3000 years.

The western boundary of Frongoch coincided with a small stream running due south about 300 yards west of Engine Shaft. Beyond, the lode passed through a different mineral ownership as far as the road down Cwm Newydion, and worked as the Wemyss Mine, generally in conjunction with Frongoch.

Trials were made on the continuation of the lode at Brook Shaft, south of Cwm Newydion Uchaf, and these workings were known as West Frongoch. The latter appellation was sometimes also applied to Wemyss, but in this account the above distinction will be observed.

The furthermost workings on the Frongoch lode were at Graiggoch, or Red Rock, Mine on the southern slopes of Cwm Newydion, about a mile from Frongoch.

Before proceeding to the history in more detail, something must be said of the geology and ore-deposits. The mining region of Cardiganshire consists of Silurian strata, which at Frongoch comprises grey or greenish-grey shales, flags and mudstones. The lodes in which the ores occur are nearly vertical faults or fractures which have become charged with deposits from mineral-bearing solutions, probably created by igneous activity at great depth in post-Carboniferous times. The exact mechanism whereby nature assembled ores in so convenient a manner is not thoroughly understood, and none who have seen a vein of shining galena sandwiched between walls of barren rock can fail to wonder at the process.

The Frongoch lode varied in width up to 30 feet, of which the galena-bearing part was not more than 24 feet and generally much less. As a rule, the ore occurred in two more or less distinct branches, referred to as the north and south part of the lode, with the blende mainly to one side of the galena. Quartz was the other constituent, and this very hard mineral rendered the lode difficult to work by hand-drilling methods. Unfortunately the productive parts became restricted laterally in depth, so that ground which paid to extract for 250 fathoms in the upper workings decreased to about 100 fathoms in the 105 and only 70 fathoms at the 130 fathom level. This, combined with increasing hardness in depth, sealed the fate of the mine.

Mineral lodes often split up and divide, and enrichment commonly takes place at junctions of this kind, again for reasons that are not clear. At Frongoch the original workings centred on an intersection at the eastern end. Frequently the galena occurred not as solid ribs, but intermingled with blende, quartz and fragments of rock, so that the whole mass required crushing and dressing in order to separate the valuable constituents.

The treatment of ores was a highly specialised process, relying largely on gravity methods of separation, and under John Taylor & Sons rose almost to the state of an art. Owing to its great density, galena was much easier to separate than blende, which could rarely be 'got up' to the same degree of purity. The very low prices sometimes obtained for second-quality blende concentrates reflected this problem. The French engineer Leon Moissenet visited the Lisburne Mines in 1860 and wrote a detailed description of the methods employed. This valuable paper is the subject of Appendix IV.

REFERENCES

1. For a general introduction, see Lewis and Bick.

2. Williams, R.A. *The Old Mines of the Llangynog District* (Sheffield: British Mining No.26, 1985).

3. Lewis, p.110

4. Lewis, p.115

5. Lewis, p.171

PART 1 – HISTORY

EARLY YEARS

The earliest reference yet discovered to mining at Frongoch is a 21-year lease dated May 30th 1759, of mines and lead ores under tenements called Frongoch, Troedyrhiw, Havod-y-rhyd and Rhiw-halog.[1,2] It was granted by Lord Lisburne to Philip Pugh of Tuglin, Cardiganshire.

Subsequently nothing has come to light until the 1790s, when John Probert began to develop Frongoch and Llwynwnwch, immediately to the east and eventually absorbed by the former. Probert was already working Fairchance, Grogwinion, Logaulas, Esgairmwyn and Esgairhir, his manager being James Lowe of Dol-y-gors.

During the year ended December 1st 1792, Lowe expended £112 for work done at Frongoch, and these extracts from his accounts give a good idea of the venture.[3]

		£.	s.	d.
To	William Hughes for opening an old level on the East End of the Workings, opening and timbering an old shaft and sumps and trenching in different parts to try for ore	2	7	6
	William Lewis, Morgan Richard, Edward Edwards, Griffith Williams, ditto...	15	3	2
	10 Lbs. Candles at 8d. per Ib		6	8
	2 Shovels at 1/9d each and 72 ft. of Boards and Rails		15	6
	2 Water Barrels at 5/- each. 1 Clivis (?)		11	0
	William Hughes raising Ore and driving Ground in the old Bottom. John Herbert, William Morgan, Evan Evans. ditto	10	4	2
	28¼ lb. of Powder, 5¼ lb. of German Steel at 6d. and 1 Quire of brown Paper, at 4d		2	11
	Joseph Dudlyke for Smith work in sharpening Tools, etc.		15	0
To	John Parry for driving a Crosscut from the Bottom of the old Work to cut the North Vein and raising Ore and Black Jack in different Parts of the two Veins to try the same - 12 weeks 2 days at 8/6d per week.	28	9	0
	John Davies, Evan Morgan, Morgan Richard, John Jones, John Roderick, Evan Shelby, John Davies, Evan John Jenkin.[4]			
To	Thomas Davies for making a new Ore Bing, and a Shed over the Knockstones for the Washers, trenching the new Vein discovered to try the Ore		11	0
	5 old Handles for Kibbles from Grogwinion Mines		3	0
	James Lowe for superintending the Mines from December 1st 1791 to December 1st 1792	20	0	0
	John Oliver for his attendance in looking after the People, delivering out stores and other sundries from 1st December 1791 to 1st December 1792 at 1/- per week.	2	12	0

From the above, the rudimentary nature of the operations is apparent, though provision of a shed for the washers (ore-dressers) is interesting. In mid-Wales, this basic protection from the worst of the weather was something of a luxury and rarely encountered.

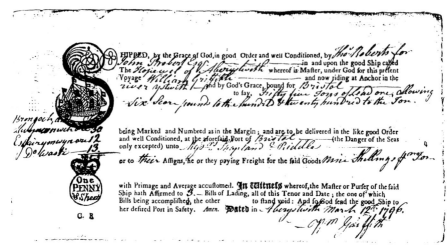

Fig.3 Bill of lading for a cargo of ore from Frongoch, Llwynwnwch and Esgairmwyn, dated March 12th 1796 (N.L.W.).

Work at Llwynwnwch had begun by August 1794, for in that month a bargain was made to raise ore in the new work at £3 15s 0d per ton of lead ore and £1 7s 6d for Black Jack.[5] John Lowe, son of James, was manager, and he frequently informed Robert Wilding, John Probert's agent, as to progress.[6]

At this time the French Revolutionary Wars were depressing prices and morale alike. In June 1795, Lowe wrote:-

> *"I have every reason to believe Llwynwnwch will make a capital concern provided it is carried on with some degree of spirit, but it cannot be done with any propriety while this ruinous War continues, and hope to God it will be brought to some conclusion before the end of the year or I don't know what will become of us except we turn Soldiers ...."*

A week later Lowe reported that Frongoch looked promising with a good rib of ore, six inches wide, intermixed with Black Jack. He went on:-

> *"I should be glad to know whether you wish to have the Llwynwnwch Ore carried down or not. The Sun impairs the colour very much, it has almost the appearance of Black Jack..."*. The observation regarding the galena is curious, and suggests it was intended for a purpose other than smelting.

Further details as to the running of the mines are that carriage of coal from Aberystwyth for the smithy cost eight shillings per ton. Timber was being hauled from as far afield as Radnorshire and gunpowder came from Shrewsbury. Unforeseen expenses also occurred, such as the cost of washing ore in

14

the storehouse at Aberystwyth which had become mixed with sand thrown up by the tide. Lead ore was only fetching £8 or £9 per ton, but nevertheless in that year Frongoch and Llwynwnwch raised about 250 tons, as far as can be judged from the records.[8]

About 1796 John Lowe and his widowed mother left Dol-y-gors and moved to Nannerth, near Rhayader. Reading between the lines of a long letter to Wilding, dated November 29th 1797, suggests that he was being edged out of his job:-[9]

> *"I hope Mr Probert through the assistance of his good friends will be as kind as to recommend me to some place or other for which I shall ever acknowledge his goodness..."*

Frongoch was struggling on, with some men able to earn ten shillings per week, but *"poor hands, who could not cut the ground as others do"* had to survive on half that reward. Much of Lowe's news was simply gossip or family matters, from which we learn that:-

> *"Old Captain Lewis of Aberystwyth has run away with his Servant maid to Ireland."*

COSTS AND RETURNS OF THE LISBURNE MINES

For *Eight Months, to the end of December,* 1834.

Date.	Lead Ores.	Amount	Lord's Dues.	Amount less Dues.	Costs.	Loss.
1834	Tons c. q.	£ s. d.	£ s. d.	£ s. d.	£ s. d.	£ s. d.
3 Months to end July.					948 18 6	
August and September					992 8 2	
3 Months to end Dec.	150 9 2	1553 17 1	188 1 10	1365 15 3	2136 5 7	
	150 9 2	1553 17 1	188 1 10	1365 15 3	4077 4 3	2711 9 0

Particulars of the Lisburne Mines Costs and Returns for Eight Months, to the end of December, 1834.

	£ s. d.		Tons cwt. q.	£ s. d.
Agents' Salaries	398 1 4	Lead Ores	150 9 2	
Tutwork Bargains	780 1 0		£1,553 17 1	
Bargains on Surface, Wages, and Stems	207 6 7	Deduct Lord's Dues	188 1 10	
Carpenters, Masons, Smiths, &c.	241 3 2			
Carriage and Whim Horses	325 15 3	Loss	2,711	
Materials	727 10 2			
Expenses on Ores	303 0 2			
Tribute Subsist and Balances	733 17 10			
Sundry Payments	360 8 9			
	£4,077 4 3			£4,077 4 3

Dr.		THE LISBURNE MINES.			Cr.
1834.		£ s. d.	1834.		£ s. d.
Aug. 4.	To paid First Instalment on account of purchase of Mines (½ of 5,000£)	1,250 0 0	June 14.	By Call on the Adventurers of 25l. per share on 100 shares	2,500 0 0
Nov. 4.	To ditto Second ditto	1,250 0 0	Sept. 16.	By Second Call ditto	2,500 0 0
	To Loss on Mines, 8 months, to end of December	2,711 9 0		Balance	211 9 0
		£5,211 9 0			£5,211 9 0

FIG. 4 Lisburne Mines cost sheet for eight months to the end of 1834.

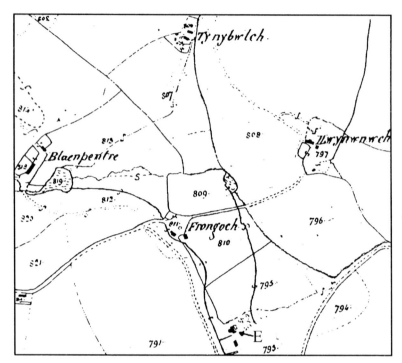

FIG. 5 The Tithe Map of 1847, showing ponds near Frongoch farmhouse and leats to the mine. 'E' marks the 1841 pumping engine (N.L.W.).

More serious was his concern that:-

> *"my Aunt Mrs Gaylor married again about 3 months ago to a young Man and has conferred all her property on him, which was £300 a year. She is upwards of 65 years of Age. I was in hopes she would have given or left the greatest part on her Decease to our family, but that is now all over..."* Life was ever thus.

Job Sheldon took over Lowe's role about the turn of the century, and during the next decade lead reached record prices. Both Frongoch and Llwynwnwch were working, and it appears that the latter was also spelt Llwynunnough, Llwynunnog and perhaps Llwynunno. Various references to these names occur.

In a letter of 1810 to Probert, Sheldon wrote:-

"I intend shipping 20 or 30 ton of Llwynunnog Black Jack by way of a trial to Harfords and Bristol Brass Co.."[10] The cargo fetched £36 15s 0d, but no more was wanted, being of too hard a quality.[11] Bristol was then a centre of the brass industry, Black Jack being used in its manufacture. The city also

imported considerable quantities of galena, and cargos from Frongoch went to Philip George, a smelter, who also owned the Patent Shot Company for making lead shot.[12]

Frongoch was still at work in 1811, but by 1816 prices had fallen heavily and two years later the mines were practically at a stand.[13] To compute their output between 1791 and 1818 is scarcely possible owing to the fragmentary records remaining. It may, however, be estimated that the two mines together raised about 3000 tons of lead ore, and a similar quantity of blende.

Following an improvement in trade, the next upturn came in 1824 when Lord Lisburne's mines were leased to a company consisting largely of the Cornish family of Williams. Those worked were Frongoch, Logaulas, Glogfach, Glogfawr, Gwaith Goch, Graiggoch or Red Rock, Penigist and Rhos Llwyd. The site of the latter is uncertain. Mines on the Gogerthan Estate were also worked, and included Cwmsymlog and Darren.[14]

Unfortunately, few details survive of the Williamses' activities. One fact worthy of recording is that in 1830 the Cornishman Robert Fox conducted pioneer experiments in Frongoch and Logaulas on electric currents generated in mineral lodes.[15] In respect of the Lisburne mines, the output figures from 1825 to 1834 clearly testify to the relative fortunes of the Williamses, and their successors and rivals, John Taylor & Sons.

THE LISBURNE MINES. Lead Ores Raised.

WILLIAMS OF SCORRIER HOUSE

YEAR	Frongoch	Logaulas	Glogfach	Glogfawr
1825	4	3	644	27
1826	24	145	42	26
1827	2	40	479	44
1828	1	157	517	13
1829	64	59	352	46
1830	216	191	359	20
1831	158	174	20	95
1832	283	136	1	32
1833	387	122	5	17
1834	258	63	14	
TOTAL	1397	959	2929	334

YEAR	Gwaith Goch	Graiggoch	Rhos Lwyd	Penygist	TOTAL
1825			3		681
1826	2	20	10	3	641
1827		43	5		613
1828	6	22			716
1829	1	6			528
1830					786
1831					447
1832					452
1833					531
1834					335
TOTAL	9	91	18	3	5730 Tons.

YEAR	Frongoch	Logaulas	Glogfach	Glogfawr	West Logaulas	Cwmdwr	TOTAL
1834	199	15		29			243
1835	807	149		211		3	1170
1836	892	420	80	73			1465
1837	671	605	19	52	23		1370
1838	447	819	129	20	62		1477
1839	78	505	17	3	93		696
TOTAL	3094	2513	245	388	178	3	6421 Tons.

It will be noted that, after an excellent start the Williamses' best mine, Glogfach, gradually went from bad to worse. Logaulas declined after 1830 and only Frongoch, after a poor beginning, was going well when the company succumbed in 1834. Whilst very high royalties of one-seventh or one-eighth and falling prices hastened the end, luck, that essential ingredient in metal-mining, was against them.

The changing fortune of Logaulas is a perfect illustration of this. In 1785 John Probert began a long adit which became known as Level Fawr or Great Level, starting above the River Ystwyth at Pontrhydygroes. The task took many years, and its sequel was chronicled by W.W. Smyth as follows:-

> "The rock was hard and the progress slow, but for upwards of 30 years did the miners persevere, till at length, after piercing about 360 fathoms, a lode was cut; but so miserable was the aspect it presented, that after driving right and left upon it for a few feet, the disappointed speculator gave up all his cherished hopes and abandoned the undertaking. After a short interval some Cornish adventurers [Williams] were led to believe that something yet remained to be done, and having set a party of men to push forward the same level, in the course of a few feet cut the true lode, in the midst of a vast deposit of ore which yielded rich returns for several years. This company, however, in their turn, fell into a similar error, and losing the true lode, mistook for it a small vein on the south, dispirited with whose poverty they surrendered the mine. The present holders, [Taylor], after making an accurate survey, were satisfied that they must be too far southward, drove a cross-cut towards the north, and very shortly discovered not only the lode, but a rich bunch of ore, parallel to which their predecessors had been toiling for many a fathom through barren rock at the distance of only a few feet. The mine has ever since been yielding several thousands of pounds profit per annum."[16]

According to Matthew Francis, the driving of Level Fawr cost £14,000 and in his opinion it was a high price to pay for something that could have been accomplished more quickly and cheaply by waterwheels for pumping.[17] At all events, the level was eventually extended to Glogfach and Glogfawr, and at its mouth were extensive dressing-floors and the headquarters of the Lisburne Mines throughout the 19th century.[18]

REFERENCES

1. Unless qualified, the word ore means lead-ore (galena)

2. N.L.W. Crosswood

3. N.L.W. Powys 1618. Meyrick in his *History of Cardiganshire* 1810, states that Frongoch consisted of 1/6 lead ore, 1/8 black jack and the rest quartz.

4. Black Jack is the old name for zinc sulphide or blende, the ore of zinc.

5. N.L.W. Powys 21939

6. N.L.W. Powys 1627

7. N.L.W. Powys 1626

8. N.L.W. Powys 1653

9. N.L.W. Powys 1733

10. N.L.W. Powys 3734. Harfords and the Bristol Brass Company lasted well into the present century. For further details, see Day, J. *Bristol Brass: A History of the Industry* (Newton Abbot: David & Charles, 1973).

11. N.L.W. Powys 4179

12. N.L.W. Powys 4203, 4156

13. N.L.W. Powys 4175

14. Lewis, 174. According to George Hall, tradition has it that Glogfawr was discovered by miners on their daily walk from Pontrhydygroes to Esgairmwyn.

15. Hunt, R. *British Mining* (1887), 390

16. Smyth W.W. *Memoirs of the Geological Survey* Vol 2. Part 2 1848, 671. When I explored Level Fawr some years ago, Smyths' story came vividly to mind, though it was not altogether borne out by evidence underground.

17. N.L.W. Druid Inn papers

18. For a section of the workings on Level Fawr see Bick, Part 1, p.31.

FIG. 6 Lisburne Mines Co. share certificate (P.J. Challis).

JOHN TAYLOR & SONS (1834-1878)

On May 1st 1834 the Lisburne Mines came into the possession of the cost-book company formed by John Taylor, who with his brothers and sons held 29 of the 100 shares.[1,2] Seven more were held by three of the Francises, a Cornish family whom Taylor employed as managers.

Taylor was then aged 54 and had proved a shrewd and capable mining engineer and promoter, with many successes to his credit. He was currently managing lead mines in Flintshire, and it would be very interesting to know what persuaded this generally cautious man to take over a group of workings in a remote part of Wales, which one of the best known mining houses in Cornwall had signally failed to master. It is true that, after years of decline, the price of lead was at least beginning to rise, but that of itself could scarcely account for his decision. Perhaps he wanted to beat the Williamses at their own game. At all events the Lisburne mines under Taylor proved a wonderful success. It is worth recording the names of the original shareholders, as extracted from the first annual report of July 1835.

LIST OF THE ADVENTURERS IN THE LISBURNE MINES

	Shares		Shares
Henry Birkbeck, Esq	5	Brought up	42
Edward Brice Bunny, Esq	5	Captain Daniel Pring, R.N.	2
Thomas Fowell Buxton, Esq	10	Captain Samuel Reed	1
Edward Chuck, Esq	2	Samuel Skinner, Esq	8
George Fossett, Esq	1	Messrs. Daniel and James Shears	2
Captain Absolom Francis	4	Thomas Stokes, Esq	10
Captain William Francis	2	John Taylor, Esq	20
Captain Matthew Francis	1	Richard Taylor, Esq	2
Charles Hopkinson, Esq	3	Edward Taylor, Esq	2
John Hutchings, Esq	1	John Taylor, Jun. Esq	3
Joseph Lyon, Esq	5	Richard Taylor, Jun. Esq	2
Charles Martineau, Esq	1	Philip Worsley, Esq	1
Colonel George Nelthorpe	2	Richard Williams, Esq	5

Shafts were often named after shareholders, e.g. Skinner's Shaft (Glogfach), Taylor's (Frongoch and Logaulas) and Worsley's (Logaulas). Philip Worsley married Taylor's eldest daughter, Anne. He was also an active partner in Whitbread's Brewery.

Matthew Francis became Taylor's resident manager of the Lisburne mines at the age of only 24. His uncle, Absalom Francis of Flintshire, had been in Taylor's employ for many years and no doubt assisted in obtaining the position.[3] The first year of operations gave very encouraging results, as may be gathered from the annual report, clear and concise, and so lacking in the hyperbole usually associated with such occasions:-

PLATE I. A general view taken in 1978. Left to right, Crusher/Winder, 1841 Engine House, 60 inch Enginehouse, c1870. Since then, the stuctures have greatly deteriorated (R.H. Bird).

THESE Mines came into the possession of the present Adventurers upon the first of May in the last year, at which time the scale of operation was a very limited one, and the returns did not exceed 40 tons of ore per month. A more spirited mode of working has been adopted, and an extension of the concern made; and it is pleasant to add that these efforts have been hitherto attended with success.

The most productive mine at present is Frongoch. The old engine-shaft, which is perpendicular and has passed through the lode, is 34 fathoms deep. A crosscut to the lode has been completed, and a level driven 7 fathoms east and 13 fathoms west of it. The ground through which it has passed was good for about 5 fathoms long, but the best ground is still before the ends. The 24 and 14-fathom levels have been extended considerable distances upon the lode, and have laid open a great deal of ground, which is working at low tributes. The old engine shaft having passed through the lode, and the crosscuts to it being long and hard, we have deemed it best to sink a new one, which is upon the underlie of the lode under the 14-fathom level. Our workings have proved this vein to be a larger and better one than we at first thought it; in places it is twelve feet wide, and turns out one and a half tons of ore per solid fathom. This mine is drained by a 40-feet water-wheel, which is supplied with water from large dams. During the last summer the works were interrupted for some time through want of water, but *by the expenditure of about £30, we have added a large additional reservoir, and improved the old ones, and shall probably not again be liable to such an impediment.*

Unfortunately, after a very good year in 1836, output fell gradually until in 1841 Taylor admitted that little benefit had accrued.[4] Lord Lisburne cut the royalty from 1/10th to 1/12th, but this did not prevent a loss announced in April 1842, mainly caused by the cost of a steam engine. A few months later Matthew Francis was sacked and replaced by Taylor's son, John Taylor jnr.

Matters now improved, partly by the acquisition of Wemyss mine to the west which was under separate ownership. The lode ran through both properties and the Wemyss adit, by extending eastwards, was made to serve both workings. The best ore occurred at the junction of two lodes, which were very productive and 30 feet wide for a length of 40 fathoms where they ran together. To the east, the main lode became impoverished and a level driven 200 fathoms proved nothing worth working. Trials west on the north lode yielded much ore, but not profitably.[5]

PLATE II. The 60 inch enginehouse, as it was in 1932. (D. Dixon).

22

PLATE III.
First aid to the 60
inch enginehouse in
1982, to prevent
collapse of the bob-
wall through rotten
wooden lintels. After
Scheduling, such
impromptu action
would have been
illegal.
(David Bick).

By 1846 Frongoch was down to the 56 fathom level with the 24 fathom level driven west as far as Boundary Shaft, beyond the road. In or about 1848 the Wemyss adit finally holed through to the 24 fathom level which then became the deep adit, the old shallow adit being only five fathoms below surface. Its site is now lost. In the Wemyss property, the adit began on the main lode near the road, but after about 150 fathoms turned north-east for about 25 fathoms before continuing eastwards on a north lode which outcrops on surface about 20 fathoms north of Boundary Shaft. A crosscut driven at this point brought the adit into the Frongoch workings.[6] Eventually the adit or 24 fathom level, with all its twists and turns, cross-cuts and exploratory drivages on parallel lodes, was extremely long. As far as can be judged from a plan c1870, it then totalled about three miles.

In 1850 annual output reached nearly 2000 tons of galena, but the year was marred by an accident when seven miners were killed by the explosion of three barrels of gunpowder, caused by the proximity of a lighted tobacco pipe.[7]

By 1851, calls on the original 100 shares had risen from an initial £25 per share to a total of £75, making a capital of £7500.

Thus far, the Lisburne mines had paid a £620 dividend on each £75 share.[8] They were run on the Tribute system where every month miners contracted to work the lode for an agreed fraction of the value of ore raised.[9] If it turned out richer than expected, the men stood to gain, but generally the dice were loaded against them. Taylor held that the method led to mining at the lowest possible cost, but it complicated the day-to-day operations since every tributer's pile of ore needed separate handling from the stopes right through to the dressing floors – an aspect that has scarcely been studied by historians and industrial archaeologists. This somewhat barbaric system of sweated labour endured almost universally to the end of the industry in Wales.

The French engineer Léon-Vivant Moissenet came to Britain to study its ore-dressing techniques and a report of his visit to the Lisburne mines in 1860 was published in great detail. It is extensively quoted in an Appendix and provides valuable information about Frongoch at its middle period. The mine was then down to the 78 fathom level with workings, including the Wemyss property, extending over ¾ mile.

Another important source is a Government enquiry into the working conditions in mines other than collieries, under the chairmanship of Lord Kinnaird.[10] In July 1863 the Commission examined Henry Thomas, general manager of John Taylor's mines in Cardiganshire, and from his evidence we learn that the mine was 103 fathoms deep, and again interrupted by a lack of water. The

24

PLATE V.
Standing above flooded stopes with the ladder to the original level of the catwalk east of Boundary Shaft; see Appendix V. (S. Timberlake).

PLATE IV. (Facing)
The 60 inch enginehouse in 1990 after the stack had blown down. Note the ruined offices beyond. (David Bick).

question of ventilation was raised, its virtues being expressed unashamedly in terms of cash.

Q. *"I suppose you find that although ventilation is a very costly matter yet in the end it is a more economical mode of proceeding"? – "Yes, unquestionably. The power of the miners is so much improved by it. You cannot get half the work from a man in an ill-ventilated place"*. The conditions of health and housing were also discussed.

Q. *As far as the miners go in this district, are they a healthy looking class of people? – They are not a healthy-looking class of people at all.*

Q. *Can you distinguish the difference between a miner and an agriculturalist? – Not always, for the agriculturalists do not look very healthy themselves.*

Q. *What are the floors of the cottages? – They are more often than not of clay and a sort of bog; you may sink into it if you sit on a chair.*

Q. *Have they fire-places? – Yes, that is their best means of ventilation, sometimes so much so that it is extremely cold.*

Q. *Are the cottages generally weather-tight? – No, I think not; that is to say the exceptions are very numerous.*

25

PLATE VI. The pit for the 56 foot waterwheel at Wemyss, used for pumping Frongoch via flat rods. Now filled in. See also plate XVII. (R.H. Bird).

Many of the miners lived several miles off, at Devil's Bridge, or farther afield, and the Taylors constructed a terrace called Miner's Row on the road to Pontrhydgroes to ease the shortage of dwellings. Many miners built cottages of their own on waste land, really little more than hovels, and with an acre or two of ground managed to scrape a little extra sustenance. Some of these memorials to forgotten endeavour, suitably improved, are still a feature of the landscape; indeed the villages of Pontrhydygroes and Yspytty Ystwyth practically owe their existence to mining. But gradually succumbing to Cardiganshire frost, wind and rain, most have sunk back into the waste from which they arose.

In 1864 new dressing floors were built at Wemyss, but two years later the deepest levels were very hard and poorer in yield. By 1868, however, Frongoch had recovered and was contributing largely to Lisburne profits.[11] In 1873 the company's agent, Thomas Ball, reported good ore on a north lode, and there was talk of sinking a new vertical shaft to cut the main lode no less than 200 fathoms below adit.[12] This idea did not last long, for the hardness of the lode in depth, plus the increased cost of working, rendered it little more than moonshine. A deep vertical shaft was much needed, however, and in 1875 Vaughan's New Shaft was begun. Taylor's Shaft (also known as Vaughan's Shaft) was down to the 142 fathom level, sunk on the dip of the lode all the way. The new shaft intersected it at the 90 fathom level.

By the mid-1870s, it was clear that Frongoch was past its best. The productive length of the lode was decreasing, working costs were rising, and ore sales were considerably down. Lead, which had remained pretty constant in price for many years, began to fall in 1877, and in 1878, after deducting royalties, Taylors made a loss for the first time since 1842. They clearly expected worse to follow, and a new lease for the Lisburne group was negotiated in which Frongoch did not number. As far as Taylors were concerned the mine as a sound proposition was finished, notwithstanding its contribution of £600,000 to profits over the past 44 years.

REFERENCES

1. N.L.W. Druid Inn Papers, Lisburne Mines Report, July 8th 1835.

2. Burt, R. *John Taylor, Mining Entrepreneur and Engineer 1779-1863* (Buxton: Moorland, 1977)

3. For biographical details of the Francis family see Bick, Part 1.

4. Jones MSS, 37

5. *M.J.* 1845, 477

6. Jones, 109

7. *M.J.* 1850, 540

8. *M.J.* 1851, 174

9. According to Simon Hughes [*The Cwmystwyth Mines* (Sheffield: British Mining No.17, 1981)], the system was in use in Cardiganshire as early as 1760.

10. H.M.S.O. Kinnaird Commission Report 1864, 504-506

11. Jones MSS, 37

12. Jones MSS, 37

PLATE VII. John Kitto, (1830-1903).

JOHN KITTO (1878-1898)

In relieving the Lisburne Mines Co. of its burden, Lord Lisburne also agreed to purchase the machinery for £5000.[1] Having acquired the mine as a going concern, he forthwith handed over the lease on July 31st 1878 at 1/20th royalty to Henry Davey and Alexander Kerby, both of London, and John Kitto of Llanidloes.[2]

The driving force behind the venture was Kitto, born in Perranzabuloe, Cornwall, in 1830. He had come to Wales from the Isle of Man in 1864 to manage the Brynpostig lead mine near Llanidloes, and many mid-Wales mines were given a new lease of life under the direction of himself and his son.[3] Few, however, achieved much success – a reflection more of exhaustion of orebodies and falling prices than of Kitto's competence as a mining engineer. And if, in promoting a company, his public trumpetings exceeded his better judgement, it was a characteristic endemic to his contemporaries and the industry as a whole. At a time when metal mining had come to be viewed as a high-risk gamble, like the Lottery, to err on the cautious side was simply to attract no capital at all. How the industry gradually succumbed to this fatal disease, akin to drug addiction, whether it might have been prevented or even cured, and to what degree its life might thus have been prolonged, are subjects of great interest which have to some extent received attention elsewhere.[4] But, we must return to matters in hand.

Having obtained the lease, Kitto passed it on to the Lisburne Syndicate Ltd, registered at 80 Cornhill, London, with a capital of £14,000 in £10 shares.[5] Of these, he held one hundred. George Ross & Co. acted as managers. The directors were Henry Davey, Thomas Kent of Southampton, and William Bowman of Middleton in Derbyshire.

On October 24th 1878 a further company, Frongoch Ltd, was incorporated to acquire the lease, plant and machinery from the Syndicate. Whatever the need for this development, John Kitto was firmly in command, with more shares than any other subscriber. The nominal capital was £25,000. George Ross acted as chairman and the directors were Bowman, Kent, and William Brookes of Hinckley. The venture was launched with the usual gusto.

According to the literature *"without any doubt this is one of the most perfect investments of its kind that has been offered to the investing public since the Van Mine was brought under their notice"*. The declining state of the lead market because of continuing imports from abroad was not mentioned, nor was the fact that the best management in the country had given up the property as beyond redemption. Nevertheless, money was quickly subscribed and work began.

A good idea of the underground state of the mine at this juncture may be gleaned from Kitto's report, dated July 1st 1878.[6] He wrote:-

"There are three principal, or main shafts for pumping and drawing, besides two or three others of less importance for ventilation, and ladder roads, the deepest of the three (which is known by the name of "VAUGHAN'S") has been sunk about 6 fathoms below the bottom, or 142-fathom level. At that depth a cross-cut has been driven through the lode from South to North, and on the latter side has intersected to be rapidly extending itself Eastwards in going down. A stope is being worked underhand here on a good course of Ore, which I value at 3 tons to the fathom.

The 142-fathom level has been driven East of Vaughan's shaft about 31 fathoms, and west 22 fathoms, principally on the South part of the lode, and near the end of the latter level there is another bunch of Ore, quite separate and distinct from the one referred to above; a stope is being worked in the back of this level upon this bunch from 6 to 8 fathoms in length, and is worth about 20 cwt of Lead Ore to the fathom. The stope in the winze at bottom of Vaughan's shaft is on the North part of the lode, but this is on the South part, and I am strongly of opinion that the North side has not been seen at, or even near this point, and that a cross-cut should be driven in that direction. The same remark applies to the level East of shaft.

The 130-fathom level has been driven from same shaft 32 fathoms East, and 45 fathoms West, and about 15 fathoms from the latter end there is a bunch of Ore on which a stope is being worked about 9 fathoms in length, and which is worth from 25 to 30 cwt of Lead Ore to the fathom. This is in whole Ground below, as the 142-fathom level has not been driven up to this point by 4 or 5 fathoms.

There are several other stopes in the various levels, but the whole of them, together with those to which I have referred, are being worked on "Tribute" at prices varying from £3 to £5 per ton of Ore, and there are many other places that could be worked at a profit with Ore selling at a fair average price. I may here remark that the stopes, to which I have referred, have yielded for some time past an average of 90 tons per month, and that this has been done without an inch of new ground being opened out, but if the deeper levels were extended, and the mine properly developed, I have no doubt that this quantity could be considerably increased. In order to secure this result, I would recommend that "Vaughan's" new perpendicular shaft should be completed and communicated with the old underlie shaft (of the same name) at the 90-fathom level, that this shaft be sunk for a new 154-fathom level as quickly as possible and simultaneously with the completing of the new part."

To conserve water in periods of drought, the usual practice allowed the bottoms temporarily to drown whilst continuing the upper workings. This at

29

PLATES VIII & IX. Two views of the opencut on the site, together with its spectacular waterfall. Through a hole near the bottom can be seen an inclined skip road in a blocked shaft and numerous stulls are in evidence (R.H. Bird).

least maintained some output, albeit at the eventual time-consuming task of raising ore and waste accumulated in the meantime.

Large stopes tended to become dangerous if not supported, and at Frongoch waste the size of coarse sand from the dressing operations was channelled down through the workings in square pipes to fill the voids. On November 24th 1879 this led to the death by suffocation of John Lewis aged 27 from a sudden run in the 117 fathom level. On February 27th 1880, a fall of ground after blasting injured the back of David Jones, aged 45. The poor man already suffered from curvature of the spine, *"the result of disease"*, and had not returned to work nearly a year later.[7]

In the summer of 1880 lack of water for pumping delayed exploration of the 154 fathom level until mid-August.[8] A crosscut had proved the lode fully 60 feet wide, but, reading between the lines, it was better in the promise than the substance.[9] A 10 per cent dividend was shortly declared, with a good improvement, worth two tons of lead ore per fathom, in the north part of the lode at the 154 east of Vaughan's Shaft. Other levels in work included the 142 and 130 west of Vaughan's (where the ground could scarcely be worked at a profit owing to its hardness), the 56, 44, 34 and 24.[10] Much blende was being raised, but at poor prices. For example, in October 100 tons fetched only £3 7s 9d per ton and 50 tons of poorer grade, £2 15s 0d. After deductions for mining, dressing, cartage and royalties, there was little profit.[11]

The Ordinary General Meeting early in 1881 tried to disguise the truth with a further 10 per cent dividend which could be ill afforded, whilst also issuing 1500 shares at £2 each to raise some floating capital. Much was made of what profits might have been, had not prices continued to fall.[12] References to potential in depth had now ceased, the 154 having failed to meet predictions. It later improved, however, and by the end of the year plans were afoot to go deeper. Practically every level in the mine was now at work with much ore revealed by further drivage and by stripping down immense reserves of blende left by the Taylors.

This was an exceptionally busy time for Kitto and his son, Frederick, who were also managing many other mines in mid-Wales, and with nothing faster than a horse for transport. The family lived in some style with two servants at Vaenor Park, Llanidloes, and afterwards at Glandwr (now St. Idloes Church Hall).[13]

Unfortunately the hardness of the lode in depth, still worked by laborious hand-drilling, proved fatal. Prospects became bleak and further demands for cash faced shareholders at the 1883 General Meeting. By 1885 things were no better, although good lead ore was reported in the 10 and 20 fathom levels east, and a new shaft was sinking from surface to the 24.[14] But, a few months later, shortage of ready cash was so serious as to prevent development of new reserves. Some idea of the parlous state of the market is revealed in the current rates for blende – 100 tons at £2 17s 9d per ton and 50 tons of lower grade at £1 12s 6d. Such prices could barely pay for stoping, far less all the other costs involved.

Towards the end of 1885, it appears that the lease passed to John Kitto himself. Regular reports to the mining press ceased and, with them, many of our sources of information.[15] But such were the resources of this renowned old mine that for a further decade ore returns hardly declined at all. Indeed, aided by a brief improvement in prices, 1888-91 yielded the highest values in the whole of Kitto's reign, with 2850 tons of blende being sold in 1888. Judging from the tramways marked on the 1st edition 25 inch Ordnance map, much of the ore came from workings at the east end, where vast opencuts revealing mineral to this day bear testimony to the amount of material removed (See Plates VIII & IX).

By 1898 Kitto was approaching 70 years old and, after a hard life was no doubt ready for retirement.[16] To what extent he gained financially from his 20 year stint is not recorded, but from 1879 to 1897 inclusive sales of ore (less royalty) totalled £180,483. Wages and other expenses amounted to £157,091, leaving a profit of £23,392. The average price gained for blende was £3 6s 0d and galena £7 10s 10d. Royalties (which were reduced to 1/30th in 1894) came to £8170.[17]

Thus the blende years had not proved entirely unsuccessful. But for Kitto it was time to go. It was also time for a younger generation with new technology to show what it could do.

REFERENCES

1. Crosswood 11, 1408

2. Crosswood 11, 1407, 1454. I suspect that Davey and Henry Davey (later of Hawthorn, Davey) inventor of the Davey Differential Steam Pump, were one and the same.

3. Bick, Part 4, 50.

4. Burt, R. *The British Lead Mining Industry* (Redruth: Dyllansow Truran, 1984).

5. P.R.O. BT31/2450/12464.

6. *Money* November 6th 1878.

7. H.M. Inspector of Mines Reports, 1879/80.

8. *M.W.* August 14th 1880.

9. *M.W.* July 17th 1880.

10. *M.W.* September 11th 1880.

11. *M.W.* October 16th 1880.

12. *M.J.* January 29th 1881.

13. 1881 Census Returns.

14. *M.J.* 1885, p.780. This may have been Orebreaker Shaft, which, according to a report by Thomas Garland dated June 6th 1903, 'was made chiefly through old workings to the 66 fathom level.' Its purpose is not clear.

15. *Mineral Statistics.*

16. In 1896 Kitto was living at Blodwen House, Aberystwyth, where he died in 1903.

17. B.G.S. Report on Frongoch, West Frongoch (Wemyss) and Red Rock mines.

FOREIGN ENTERPRISE

It was symptomatic of the industry that as long as money could be found, old mines were never allowed to die. Instead, they were kept alive or even resurrected by a series of financial injections, as if by some miracle the laws of economics might be reversed. Indeed, aided by the gullibility of investors, such promotions are by no means unknown in this country today.

Such were the circumstances behind the last great working of Frongoch. The company initially involved was a Belgian firm of lead smelters from Liège, the Société Anonyme Minière, and it leased Frongoch and Red Rock (Graiggoch) from November 18th 1898 for a period of 42 years. The annual rent was £230, together with a complicated royalty based on a sliding scale of market prices, which, with lead at £14 per ton, came to about 1/40th of the value of the ore.[1]

In spite of a huge investment in modern machinery, the venture proved a failure, and its course was recalled by the ex-manager, George Trefois, shortly after work ceased.

"The Plant [inherited from Kitto] *was antiquated and worked only at a high cost. The Société Minière being satisfied from the reports of excellent experts that the property could yield very large quantities of a very good Zinc and Lead Ore, immediately started erecting a modern Plant to obtain a high output and reduce the working costs.*

The principal Shafts were repaired and re-timbered, also the levels and footways. The previous Companies worked principally the east part of the Mine between Edwards' and Pryce's Shafts. They found there a very rich chute [sic] *in which they sank down to 154 fathoms. This part of the Mine was considered as practically exhausted down to the 90 fathom level which was the deepest worked by the Société Minière. Therefore the first trials were made on the Eastern continuation of the lode: 400 fathoms of virgin ground remain before the boundary of the lease is reached. These trials led by a local Captain were made without the necessary push and perseverance. Efforts were spread on many points instead of concentrating on one, and it is true to say that this exploration Eastwards remains entirely to be done.*

The price of metal at that time (1896-1899) being very satisfactory, the Société's immediate aim was to obtain a sufficient output to take advantage. This could be got best from the Western part; the old levels and passes gave a basis to open Blende stopes in a district where Lead only had been worked to some extent. The Western part between Vaughan Shaft and Boundary Shaft was immediately prepared, and stopes gradually started.

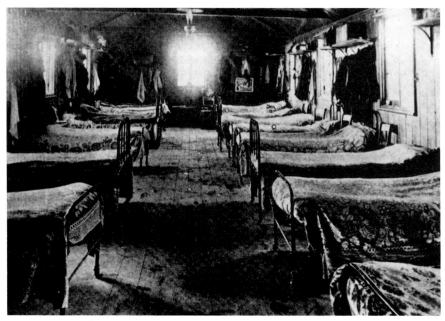

PLATE X. *The barracks at Frongoch, c1900. The building was afterwards moved to Cwmystwyth (S.J.S. Hughes).*

In the meantime there arose a good opportunity to purchase the neighbouring Mine, West Frongoch [Wemyss]. The capital of the Société Minière being fully invested in other ventures - Rosas, Lakamody, Gra-Roubon, etc., the Frongoch Mine and Plant were sold [in 1899] to the Société Anonyme des Mines de Frongoch with a profit of £8000. This latter Company purchased West Frongoch and continued working the West part of Frongoch. Till recently it can be said that practically all the crude Ore wound to the surface came from this district, about 35,000 tons. The working costs were low but the yield in concentrates was not high enough (slightly over ten per cent) and with the prices of metals which ruled then (1901 and 1902) it did not pay.

It was then resolved to try the pillars left in the North-East chute, and to open up the continuation of this chute between the 78 fathoms and 90 fathom levels. The yield was found to be very good: twenty to twenty-five percent of concentrates; but the working costs were high on account of the hardness of the ground. Three Gradner Electric Drills were tried, but did not give all the expected results. The installation of Air Drills was no doubt advisable, but the Société hesitated spending the necessary capital for this new Plant, and all work in the Mines was stopped in December 1902.

However, the Dressing Mill was kept going day and night with the dumps from the old Mine and this left a satisfactory margin of profit. A few men were kept prospecting in the 90 fathoms E. and the 66 fathoms W. and their discoveries altered favourably the prospects of the venture. But the Shareholders had definitely decided not to finance the undertaking any more, and put the Société in liquidation on the 15th June 1903. The Mill worked the dumps up to the 10th August. The Machinery and Plant were sold to Messrs. R.A. King & Company on the 20th November 1903.''

It was the old story bringing its inevitable conclusion, but nevertheless it was one which, with better management and foresight, might have been postponed.

The most remarkable feature concerned the wholesale replacement of plant and machinery by the latest electrically-driven equipment, as is described later. To what extent this investment actually reduced working costs, to say nothing of interest on capital, may much be doubted, however. Old-fashioned hand-drilling proved the heaviest burden, but, at a time when compressed-air drills were being rapidly introduced elsewhere, such developments were strangely ignored.

Metal prices improved in 1898, but they held only for a year or two. Unfortunately production did not get into its stride until 1902, with 426 tons of lead ore and 2726 tons of blende, much of which, it appears, came from

PLATE XI. A view down the incline to the new mill, showing the bridge under the road (R.H. Bird).

the old dumps.[2] Even so, Kitto had equalled or beaten these figures on several occasions, antiquated machinery notwithstanding. Indeed, in 1888 his output of 310 tons of lead ore and 2850 tons of blende had been achieved with a total labour force of only 147, including women - some 88 fewer than employed in 1902, as noticed below.[3] Kitto himself died in 1903, and it was perhaps appropriate that the mine, which he had struggled to turn into profit for 20 years, did not survive him.

In some respects the management seems to have gone out of its way to jeopardise the chances of success. The problems were much compounded by the cosmopolitan nature of the venture, involving Belgian capital, British, French and German machinery, and a Welsh and Italian labour force. The latter inevitably invited clashes of race and creed, to say nothing of language and communication difficulties. To the Italian miner, rural Cardiganshire at the turn of the century must have seemed as remote as the moon, and hardly more hospitable. According to the late R.R. Nancarrow of Pontrhydgroes, the immigrants' arrival led to a nine month strike, and on November 24th 1900 the *Mining Journal* reported:-

> *"For the past week disturbances have taken place at the Frongoch lead mine, Aberystwyth, which is worked by a Belgian company. At these mines 250 Welshmen are employed with 200 Italians, and since the foreigners were imported there has been trouble. The disputes which have arisen during the past 10 days have been of a serious character, necessitating the presence of county police day and night, the tact of Chief-constable Evans alone keeping the Welsh miners in check. The managers were readily disposed to argue the question out, but the police were, nevertheless, compelled to guard the Italians to and from the mines."* [4]

In addition, when several Italians became unwell, alarm arose lest they should have unwittingly introduced ankylostomiasis, or miner's anaemia, to the area.[5] The Government Inspector, Dr C. Le Neve Foster, submitted samples for bacterialogical examination, but the fears proved groundless. In the same report he commended the Belgian company for providing accommodation *"far ahead of that which prevails in some parts of Wales"* – an allusion to men sleeping two in a bunk with straw for a mattress.

Other factors contributing to the mine's collapse were the erection of a 20 ton per hour mill without sufficient equipment underground to feed it, and inadequate sliming plant, so that half the values were lost.[6]

Shortly before closure, Thomas Garland of Laxey made a thorough inspection of the workings above the 90 fathom level, from which it was abundantly clear that precious little ore remained in sight. In his opinion, the best prospects lay in trying the lode beyond disturbed ground east of the mine, but the advice was never followed.[7]

The fundamental problem, however, was the weakness of the market, and we can easily guess the response to this pathetic little advertisement that appeared in the *Mining Journal* for August 1903:-

> *"Blende mine for sale in Wales, four miles from Station in steady working. Mineral of excellent quality. Well equipped with Ore Dressing machinery of latest type, all motivated by Waterpower."*

The period may be summarised as follows:-[8]

| Year | Numbers employed | | | Ore Returns (tons) | | Manager |
	Surface	U/ground	Total	Lead	Zinc	
1898	70	88	158	201	1649	Max Stegemann
1899	133	95	228	43	549	B. Nogara
1900	125	145	270	42	663	G.H. Trefois
1901	90	69	159	333	1739	"
1902	120	115	235	426	2726	"
1903	?	?	?	202	1453	"
				1247	8479	

PLATE XII. The new mill at Wemyss Mine (R.H. Bird).

REFERENCES

1. N.L.W. The Crosswood Estate (Thesis) J.M. Howells 1956, 398

2. B.G.S. J. Trefors, Report on the Frongoch Mines

3. H.M. Inspectors of Mines Reports.

4. The total of 450 employees is suspect. The *Mineral Statistics* records only 270 for 1900 and fewer in other years.

5. For details of this disease at British mines,

see Boycott & Haldane, "Ankylostomiasis" *Journal of Hygiene*, (January 1904).

6. B.G.S. R.R. Nancarrow, Report to Capt. J.M. Carey, H.M. Inspector of Mines September 20th 1939.

7. Report held by B.G.S.

8. H.M. Inspectors of Mines Reports and Mineral Statistics.

SCRAPING THE BARREL

The final chapter hardly concerns mining as such. It is in great measure the story of how the enormous waste-dumps were removed and treated for lead and zinc which hitherto had been deemed scarcely worth the cost of recovery. Although this development did not begin until the demand for metals rose during the First World War, the company involved was the Lisburne Development Syndicate, formed in 1907.

The Syndicate began operations at Glogfawr, where a practically virgin north lode was profitably exploited.[1] The manager was R.R. Nancarrow, who, at the age of 24, supervised construction of the Davey Shaft by simultaneously rising from the 90 fathom level (Level Fawr) and sinking from surface.[2] Such a project called for the utmost precision in surveying under difficult conditions, and its successful outcome confounded the sceptics, who numbered the great majority.

By 1917 the Glogfawr north lode was almost worked out, and the company turned to Gwaithgoch in the Ystwyth valley south of Frongoch.[3] Blende and galena were fetching excellent prices, and good ore was reported in winzes sunk below No.3 level, to be worked by a projected deep adit. The Frongoch dumps also attracted attention, and the Lisburne Development Syndicate proposed an aerial ropeway from them to the Gwaithgoch Mill, with access by a long timber bridge over the River Ystwyth. Nancarrow planned the whole operation, including a new leat to convey the waters of the river to a turbine at the mill. In September 1919 William Thomas, late head of the mining department of the Camborne School of Mines, reported as follows:-[4]

> "A scheme for working GWAITH-GOCH MINE had been prepared before the national necessity arose for the increase of home production of zinc and lead ores to meet war requirements. That necessity, together with your acquisition of FRONGOCH DUMPS made it desirable to amend the original GWAITH-GOCH scheme. This has been done.
>
> The FRONGOCH DUMPS contain about 150,000 tons of lodestuff, which will pay handsomely for treatment at present prices for zinc and lead, the average dump contents having been ascertained to run 5% blende with One ton of galena per 10 tons of blende. These dumps accumulated in the earlier part of the last century, when FRONGOCH was a rich lead mine and blende was thrown aside as waste.
>
> An aerial Ropeway has been constructed from FRONGOCH to GWAITH-GOCH mill-site, a distance of 3050 yards. The mill house has been erected and concrete foundations practically completed for a well designed crushing and dressing plant which is ready for immediate delivery.

PLATE XIII. Flotation cells near Vaughan's New Shaft c1958. (S.J.S. Hughes).

At the present time about £12 per ton is obtainable for blende concentrates of 50% zinc. At this price and with a recovery of 85%, ensured by the inclusion in the dressing plant of an efficient floatation unit as proposed, the dumps will yield a profit of between £40,000 and £50,000 under existing conditions and calculating for current rate of labour and prices of materials.

A Dam 28 feet high by 120 feet in length at the top has been built across the YSTWYTH RIVER and a water-course 2400 yards in length, is under construction. This will convey a sufficient volume of water from the Dam to provide 200 b.h.p. by means of a turbine near the mill site. In addition to providing the necessary power for crushing and dressing, the turbine will also suffice for pumping, hoisting and indeed for all power demands at GWAITH-GOCH MINE. I have carefully examined all the details of the scheme and am satisfied that it meets all the requirements of the case.''

In the winter of 1919/20 control passed to a new company, the Welsh Mines Corporation Ltd, with the Earl of Lisburne as chairman and Nancarrow as general manager. It acquired mineral rights over 2500 acres, including Gwaithgoch and the Frongoch dumps, and a year later a correspondent of the mining press described the operations.[5,6]

"At Frongoch two reservoir pools are a source of power for the Pelton wheel which drives the mechanical haulage and the machinery at the sorting station. The lode-stuff from the dumps is raised into a portable bin by a 'Priestman' steam crane grab, from whence it is conveyed by a mechanical haulage to the elevated sorting station, which is equipped with storage bins having a total capacity of 240 tons. At this sorting station a large portion of the debris is discarded and the mineral conveyed by means of a ropeway (of Messrs Ropeways, London) to the mill. The ropeway has a maximum capacity of 15 tons per hour and extends across valleys and down mountain-sides, constituting a most interesting and picturesque sight. Of the buckets that pass along this ropeway, at the time of our correspondent's visit, 66 were operating, each holding about 3 cwt. On arrival at the mill, the ore is dumped into storage bins. The mill itself is of modern construction and is capable of treating about 7½ tons per hour. It is contained in a building where everything has been arranged for the utmost economy in treating the produce. The ore, passing down through various stages of sizing, crushing, classifying, separation and concentrating, is untouched by hand from the moment it enters the stonebreaker until the dressed mineral is weighed."

PLATE XIV. August, 1971. A borehole put down to a depth of over 800 feet proved little mineralisation. (David Bick).

Unfortunately the plant was not ready for production before metal prices fell on release of government stock-piles after the war. Blende became virtually unsaleable and it was, therefore, decided to produce metallic zinc on the spot by means of electrolysis. The process had been developed within the past few years, and was not without its teething troubles. Attempts to obtain a loan under the Trade Facilities Act met with a very guarded response from a consultant, and the idea does not appear to have come to fruition.[7]

In 1923 the Lisburne Development Syndicate and the Welsh Mines Corporation amalgamated under the control of the Cambrian Electrolytic Zinc Co. and Nancarrow continued as manager. Treatment of the dumps began, but prices had not recovered sufficiently and the Debenture Holders put the new company into the hands of the Receiver. The assets were sold to the Western Mining Co. and production continued until low prices forced a final suspension. According to Nancarrow, from 1924 to 1930 over 51,000 tons of low grade lead/zinc ores from Frongoch dumps were treated by flotation, yielding some 6000 tons of blende and 600 tons of galena concentrates.[8]

In 1929 Nancarrow re-examined Frongoch above adit level.[9] Some twenty years afterwards, the late Mr Dandrick of Cwm Rheidol acquired the Lisburne mineral rights and set up a small dressing plant near the New Vaughan Shaft for blende concentration. He started a level from the shaft about 60 feet down towards the lode, but it does not appear that these endeavours led to any production. Since then, depressed prices and other factors discouraged further attempts, although a deep borehole was drilled in 1971.

REFERENCES

1. Manager's Report, August 10th 1908. (In possession of G.W. Hall.)

2. Information from G.W. Hall.

3. *M.W.* September 29th 1917.

4. Report to Directors, September 1st 1919 (In possession of G.W. Hall.)

5. *M.W.* January 8th 1921.

6. The ropeway ran almost dead-straight, its course being shown on contemporary One-inch Ordnance Survey maps.

7. B.G.S. F.W. Harbord, 'Report on the Recovery of Zinc ... by Electrolysis' 1922

8. R.R. Nancarrow, 'Synopsis of Mining Career' March 20th 1945. It must be observed that the yield seems suspiciously high (In possession of G.W. Hall.)

9. Hall recalls that Nancarrow told him that, as a leg-pull, he had suggested to O.T. Jones extending the Level Fawr at Grogwinion (west of Gwaithgoch) a mile or more to Frongoch to provide a deeper adit. The professor not only approved, but put the idea forward in print. (Jones, p.107).

PLANT AND MACHINERY

Tramlines, slag heaps and pieces of machinery,
That was, and still is, my ideal scenery.
W.H. Auden

More than a century of almost continuous activity witnessed countless changes and modifications to the machinery, to say nothing of numerous experimental developments. From rudimentary beginnings, almost every phase of mining technology was passed through, culminating in the latest state of electrical power engineering at the close of the 19th century.

Pumping burdens nearly every mine, but those in the clay-slate rocks of Wales were not generally very wet. Provided surface water was excluded as far as possible, small workings could reach considerable depths by manual pumping alone, or by raising water in a barrel with the ubiquitous horse-whim. Nevertheless, this was only achieved by relentless and often exhausting labour, which may be better appreciated by the realization that a flow of no more than a kitchen tap amounts to 15 or 20 tons in weight every 24 hours.

At Frongoch it appears that these primitive methods sufficed until the Williams' era, 1825-34, for no mention has been found of an engine-shaft or any form of mechanical pumping before that time.

But however detrimental water proved below ground, its presence above was indispensable. Waterwheels were common in nearly every Welsh mining district and, fed by long leats from storage ponds, were the equivalent of the modern electric motor and grid system.

Unfortunately, being on a plateau, Frongoch was poorly situated. The small catchment area set a definite limit on the power attainable, no matter how many storage ponds might be constructed, and proved a major restriction on the rate of output. Theoretically at least, the ample headwaters of the Mynach east of Devil's Bridge could have been brought to the mine, and, in view of the Taylors' long leats elsewhere, one wonders why it was never done.

An early reference to waterpower occurred in June 1795, when John Lowe wrote: *"The Stamps are quite at a stand owing to the scarcity of water occasioned by the present Drought. Most of the Springs are quite dry...."*[1] It was a cry endlessly repeated. When John Taylor & Sons took over in 1834, the mine was drained by a 40 foot waterwheel and it was prophecied that a new reservoir would render an adequate supply for all seasons. Hitherto, with regard to crushing the ore, there is little doubt that stamps had provided the only mechanized means. But, although more effective than manual methods, stamps tend to produce an excessive amount of fines. Taylor had introduced crushing-rolls to his lead mines elsewhere, as these were better adapted for the primary treatment of such ores.[2] Rolls were soon at work at

PLATE XV. The Generating Station, with Red Rock Mine and the leat from Wemyss in the background (R.H. Bird).

Frongoch, for Absalom Francis wrote from Halkyn to his nephew, Matthew, on January 31st 1838: *"I have noticed your sketch for decreasing the speed of the Frongoch rollers and will order the necessary things to be sent with the next vessel direct from this place to Aberystwyth."*[3]

Within a year or two water shortage was again apparent. Steam seemed the only solution and, from his experience in Cornwall, Taylor determined to introduce it here. In April 1841 he wrote informing his manager, Matthew Francis, of the appointment of James Morcom as engineer to his Cardiganshire mines. *"Your uncle* [Absalom Francis of Flintshire] *has recommended him strongly ... I suppose his principle attention will be directed to the erection of the Frongoch Engine ..."* The machinery came by coaster from the Taylors' Rhydymwyn foundry in Flintshire.

In the Lisburne Mines report for June 1841, shareholders were informed of the new development and must have learned with some surprise that the engine was to pump water from adit-level for re-circulation over the waterwheels - an application reverting a century to the days of Thomas Newcomen.[4] But, although inefficient, it could be simply applied and, short of drastically re-designing the plant, nothing else was feasible.

The total fall over the wheels amounted to 16 fathoms or nearly one hundred feet. They comprised two for pumping, 44 and 20 foot diameter, and one for a crusher and jigging machine, 18 foot diameter. A special shaft, the exact site of which is now uncertain, was sunk from surface to adit to accommodate a lift of 24 inch diameter pumps for the purpose.

In April 1842 it was admitted that the cost of the engine and its erection had involved a loss of £3246 on the year's working. Great benefits were needed to justify such an outlay, but none came. After only a few years of occasional use, the experiment was abandoned with the 40 in. x 9 ft. stroke engine advertised in February 1847 for £650, with boilers extra at £12 per ton.

Within a few months Frongoch was once more inundated, and the deserted engine house prompted an embarrassing correspondence in the *Mining Journal*. One contributor volunteered the information that an hydraulic engine was shortly to be applied. This was a Darlington water-pressure engine with two 20 inch cylinders of six foot stroke. These worked like a steam engine, and a similar one with 24 inch cylinders was built at Cwmystwyth.[5]

However, since no further reference can be found, we may suspect problems, and certainly one installed at Minera lead mines near Wrexham in 1851 was less than successful.[6] Nonetheless, these engines were quite in vogue at the Taylors' mines in the 1840s and 1850s.

At which of the Frongoch shafts the Darlington engine was fitted is unknown. It may well survive, and its discovery would no doubt cause a sensation, as when a similar machine came to light at the Alport mines, Derbyshire, some 15 years ago.

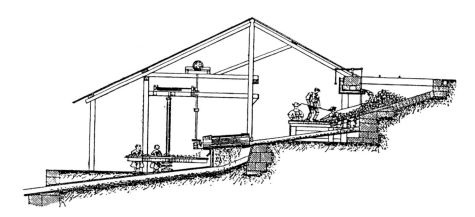

FIG. 7. On the dressing floors, c1860. A wash-kiln, sizing trommel and hand-sorting or picking table. (R. Hunt).

At all events, interruptions continued. After a visit in 1860, the French engineer Léon Moissenet wrote:-

"The motive power of the Lisburne mines is entirely hydraulic, an almost vital condition in a locality where coal costs 25 shillings per ton ... At Frongoch to guard against want of water, recourse has been had to vast reservoirs; the principle wheel is used for pumping; it is not less than 55 feet diameter and 4 feet 6 inches wide, and estimated at 60 horse power ..."

The reservoirs included the old ones in the valley above Frongoch, and two big ponds in the hills to the north-west, Rhos-rhydd and Glan-Dwgan.

When the Kinnaird Commission took evidence in July 1863 Frongoch was again idle, with the desperate remedy of steam once more in contemplation. In the summer of 1867 the railway station opened at Crosswood, only four miles from the mine. The prospect of cheaper coal may well have swung the balance, for two engines were erected, one being a 60 inch x 11 foot stroke for pumping at Engine Shaft, the other a 25 inch rotative for drawing (winding) and crushing at Taylor's Shaft. The 60 inch engine came from Sandicroft Foundry and the large heap of grass-grown cinders, still extant, testifies to its labours over the years.

Moissenet's detailed description of the dressing floors also leaves one with no doubt that they represented the best technology of the time.

When new management took over Frongoch in 1878, extensive changes followed. The plant and equipment it inherited is given in detail by an inventory accompanying the new lease.[7] Although somewhat garbled, it gives a good impression of the scale of operations and is reproduced in full.

SCHEDULE

One 30' x 3' 6" waterwheel, one 56' x 5' waterwheel with crank and balance-bob. One 26' x 7' waterwheel, drawing-machine to ditto. One 20' x 3' waterwheel, crusher to ditto. One 20' x 2' waterwheel, rockbreaker and gearing to ditto. One 12' x 2' waterwheel (undershot) driving three riddles and round tables and including shafts and gearing. Two waterwheels for driving collieries jiggers and coal rake. One 30⁻ x 3' old waterwheel, drawing-machine attached. Six small waterwheels on the flooring and at Smith's shop. One 14' x 14" waterwheel, 3 collars jiggers with gearing, one coal rake ditto, two Zennor buddles ditto, 9 round buddles ditto, six handjiggers. Crushing mill connected to steam engine, drawing-machine ditto. Sheds throughout the mine, three shaft tackles, five pullies, timber etc.

One shears at the pumping-engine, two balance-bobs, 220 fathoms ⁹/₁₀ chain 18 lbs per fathom 2 tons, 150 fathoms 1¹/₈" wire rope 9 lbs per fathom 11 cwts, 100 fathoms estimated of another piece 12 cwts. 252 fathoms 3 inch round iron rods 143 lbs per fathom 16 tons, 120 fathoms 2 inch rod, 63 lbs per fathom 3½ tons. Pullies and stands under rods say 60 in number, pullies 1¼ each 75 Ibs, woodwork £20. Pulley stands under chain and wire rope say 120 fathoms, lines 20 stands pullies 12 cwts woodwork £10. Pulley-stands, weighbridge, smith's shop, two bellows, anvils, tools say 10 cwts. Rails at surface including pond 810 fathoms double 16lbs per yard 23 tons. Rails underground 1850 fathoms single, 3630 double at 16 lbs per yard 50 tons, old scrap and cast-iron, worn out pit-work, old chains, iron in balance-boxes etc say 45 tons, a number of tram wagons at surface and underground.

In shafts – Vaughan's [Taylor's]
One 8" bucket lift 12 fathoms long say 3 tons, one 10" plunger lift 23 fathoms long say 9 tons, one spare 9" bucket lift 12 fathoms long, 23 fathoms or 138 foot run of 8" square rods say 60 feet cube, strapping plates and connections to ditto 10 cwts iron, other things, round iron rods to surface 1½'' to 2½'' say 2½ tons, balance and angle-bobs, skip-road 6 inches and 5 inches, from bottom of Vaughans shaft to surface 160 fathoms say 420 feet cube.

Engine Shaft
From the 56 fathom level to the 24 fathom level 16" plunger lift 32 fathoms long 21 pipes each 9ft long 336 cwts, plunger case 16 cwts add 'H' piece and say 20 tons. From the 90 fathom level to the 56 fathom level 15" plunger lift 31 fathoms long, 21 pipes at 15 cwts each and other parts say 18 tons. From the 117 fathom level to the 90 fathom level 12" plunger lift 28 fathoms long, 19 pipes at 12 cwts each with plunger case say 13 tons.

52 fathoms or 312ft 14" square rods	*424 cu.ft.*
31 fathoms or 186ft 12" square rods	*186 cu.ft.*
52 fathoms other rods to surface	*312 cu.ft.*
28 fathoms or 168ft 10" square rods	*116 cu.ft.*
	1038 cu.ft.

Strapping plates, bobs etc say 6 tons, balance bob at 44 fathom level, fend-off bobs etc, skip-road from 90 fathom level to surface say 120 fathoms or 720 feet, 300 fathoms (computed) of ladders. At surface, pipes about sufficient to make up 2 lifts at 15 fathoms each.

Steam Engines
One 60" cylinder pumping engine with 2 boilers, one 25" cylinder drawing and crushing engine and 1 boiler, sundries reservoirs sluices, leats etc.

The inventory raises queries such as the purpose of '*collars jiggers and coal rake*', but also throws light on the pumping arrangements and machinery. It

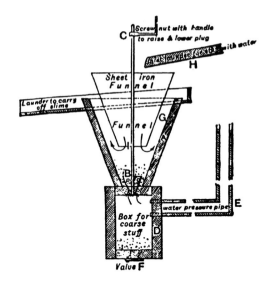

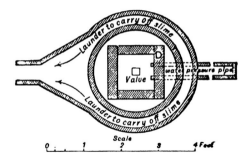

FIG. 8 A separating table c1890 (C. Le Neve Foster).

appears that 8 and 10 inch pumps in Vaughan's (Taylor's) Shaft raised water from the bottoms only about 35 fathoms, from whence the larger steam pumps at Engine Shaft brought it to the adit or 24 fathom level, together with water from the upper parts of the mine. Thus, even with steam, in times of drought the workings could only be kept dry down to the 105.

Of the waterwheels, the 26 foot example working a drawing machine (winding drum) calls for comment, being of no less than seven foot breast. Such a width implies an unusually large flow of water, which in turn suggests re-circulation by some means or another, akin to the experiments with steam in 1841. The 56 foot wheel was at Wemyss, west of the road, to which a long and circuitous leat conveyed water from the dressing floors. It presumably replaced the 55 foot wheel recorded by Moissenet. Its impressive wheelpit still survives, although largely filled in (See Plate VI).

47

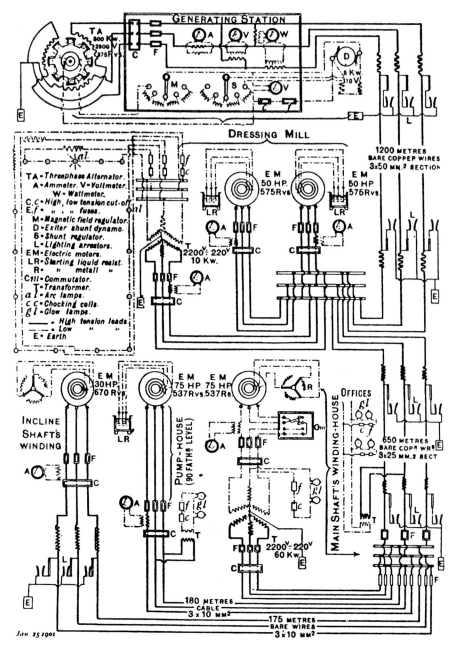

Fig. 9. Frongoch electrical circuit, 1901. (E.H. Davies).

PLATE XVI. Inside the Generating Station. (R.H. Bird).

One of John Kitto's first moves was to fix a line of rods from the Wemyss wheel to Vaughan's New Shaft. By June 1879, he had applied 24 inch pumps to recirculate water over the wheel, apparently as a kind of perpetual motion device, which was reported to work exceedingly well.[8]

Winding arrangements at Frongoch had advanced a long way from the horse-whim and kibble, but, via Richard Trevithick, one of Kitto's improvements is directly traceable to that time-honoured machine. Robert Hunt relates an amusing tale from the early years of the 19th century when Trevithick constructed a much larger kibble for the new steam whims. The winding wheels were raised so that the kibble might go higher, whereupon the landing-man exclaimed, *"I wonder who is going to land them big kibbles, I shan't land them."* Captain Trevithick replied *"Can't you wait a bit?"* When it was all complete, the kibble did not need landing. It turned upside down, and the stuff fell directly into the wagon.[9] The system was not, however, entirely automatic.

Vaughan's New Shaft was completed to the 154 fathom level by the summer of 1879, the last 64 fathoms extending the old shaft which followed the dip of the lode. It was fitted with a double skip, which ran on wooden guide-rails. To develop Trevithick's ideas further, the rope was not fixed to the top of the skip but to the bottom, which, together with an ingenious geometry of the guide-rails in the head-frame, enabled the skip automatically to invert itself, and discharge. According to Le Neve Foster, this simple and elegant device was due to Captains Kitto, Paul and Nancarrow.[10]

To make the best returns from blende which Messrs Taylor had largely ignored, revision of ore-dressing practice was essential, and we are fortunate in having detailed descriptions of some of the new plant.[11,12] The run-of-mine ore was sized as before by gratings and trommels, and girls using revolving picking-tables separated the material by hand into three sorts. These were (1) pure blende and galena, (2) a mixture of blende, galena and rock, and (3) waste rock. Figure 7 is an illustration of the building and plant.[13]

The fine material went straight to the jiggers, while the larger sizes were put through crushing-rolls and graded by another device called a Separator.[14] In the diagram (Fig.8), water under pressure flowed up from the box D into the conical chamber A, into which the launder H brought the product from the crusher. The upward current carried the light and fine material away, while the coarse and heavy constituents sank and were removed through the valve F. The jigger for separating galena, blende and waste rock was an oblong box in which a wooden board, acting as a piston, moved on a horizontal axis between two compartments.[15] The motion came from a crank driven by a waterwheel, and the device worked in somewhat similar principle to the separator. Whether Kitto and his colleagues also devised these appliances is an interesting question, and probably has an affirmative answer.

But the limitations of waterpower were still very much apparent, as both engines were again reported in steam at the 1881 AGM.[16] In a further attempt at salvation, Kitto erected another big wheel for winding, if not for pumping also. It was located alongside a big disused crusher-house and above Orebreaker Shaft and worked a drawing-machine with a five foot diameter drum via spur gears and belts. From the 1904 sale catalogue, Orebreaker Shaft had a wooden headframe with seven foot diameter sheave, apparently worked from the above drum, but this, however, was by no means aligned on it. (See Front Cover). Presumably the ropes passed round pulleys in a horizontal plane to change their direction nearly 90° - an unusual arrangement. The new wheel called for a greater head of water and the leat system was altered to provide it.

The next major change in the plant and machinery was as imaginative as it proved misguided. On taking over Frongoch in 1898, the Société Anonyme Minière determined to grasp the nettle with a strong, not to say fatal, dose of modern technology. Under a young Italian electrical engineer named Nogara, the old waterworks were ruthlessly supplanted by electric motors energised from a cathedral-like power-station a mile to the west.[17] It contained a 2300 volt A.E.G. alternator, driven by a 400 h.p. Escher-Wyss Pelton Wheel operating under a 400 foot head and supplied by three existing reservoirs. One of these was the old Frongoch Pool, and three miles of leat were dug to convey its waters to the small header pond high above the power station. In the event of drought, a 360 h.p. Willans & Robinson six cylinder compound steam engine, complete with Babcock & Wilcox boilers, was also provided.[18] The more things changed, the more they stayed the same.

New dressing-floors were built at Wemyss mine and fed from Vaughan's New Shaft by half-a-mile of chain-operated tramway which passed under the road in a cutting. In essentials, the mill comprised two stone-breakers, crushing rolls 30 x 16 inch by Green of Aberystwyth and 21 x 12 inches by Krom. There were also numerous trommels and elevators, 16 jigs by Green and sundry vanners and other plant too numerous to itemize. Various electric motors had marble switch-boards and liquid starting resistances, with some of the smaller machines being run on 220 volts via a transformer.[19]

Similar extravagance applied at the mine, where at Vaughan's New Shaft Fraser & Chalmers erected a 60 foot high lattice girder headframe with eight foot diameter sheaves. A corrugated-iron shed housed a 125 h.p. motor by Pinette of Chalons-sur-Sâone with gear reductions to the winding drum. It is not without a certain dry amusement to record that, in the midst of all the latest technology, one spur-wheel had cogs of apple-wood, with ample spares provided, in the best tradition of the medieval mill-wright. There were also 80 h.p. and 75 h.p. motors by A.E.G. and a 30 h.p. for winding at Edwards' Shaft. The mine never worked below the 90 fathom level, from which depth an underground, electrically-driven pump operated. However, according to a report by John Mitchell, towards the end it was relieved of its duty by an old-fashioned water-wheel.[20] The wheel of destiny had turned full circle.

As to the total cost of the plant and machinery, there are conflicting accounts. E.H. Davies, a well-known mining engineer and a friend of Nogara, put the figure at £10,000.[21] Mitchell quoted £45,000 – a much more probable sum, though even this may not have included labour. At all events, the five-day sale in 1904 recouped but a tiny fraction of the capital invested.

In view of the electrification, the waterwheels at Frongoch must in general have been redundant for years, and from the 51 page catalogue the list appended below makes an illuminating comparison with that of 1878.

1878		1904	
56 x 5ft	Pumping	50 x 4ft.	Drawing
30 x 3ft 6in.		29 x 3ft. 6in.	
30 x 3ft	Drawing	26 x 6ft.	Drawing
26 x 7ft	Drawing	12 x 1ft.	Blacksmith's Shop
20 x 3ft	Crushing	2 unspecified	
20 x 2ft	Rockbreaker		
14 x 14ins			
12 x 2ft undershot			
8 unspecified			

51

It appears that, apart from the 26 x 6 foot example which may equate with the 26 x 7 foot of 1878, not a single wheel from the earlier period had survived. Furthermore, the altered range of diameters suggests not so much a replacement of old by new, but a thorough re-design of layout and surface arrangements during the Kitto period. This is confirmed by the layout of the mine-buildings.[22]

Also sold was a brand-new pitchpine headframe at Ball's Shaft, *"cut, jointed and partly framed, but never erected."* At the offices could be bought an eight-day clock in a mahogany case, and a miner's dial. Altogether a pathetic end to a brave, but misguided, venture.

REFERENCES

1. N.L.W. Powys 1626.

2. For further details of 19th century ore-dressing, see Burt, R. *A Short History of British Ore Preparation Techniques in the Eighteenth and Nineteenth Centuries* (Lelielaan: De Archaeologische Pers, 1982).

3. N.L.W. Druid Inn papers.

4. In the 1740s, a Newcomen engine powered ten waterwheels at Coalbrookdale in this manner. See - Farey, J. *A Treatise on the Steam Engine* 2 volumes (Newton Abbot: David & Charles, 1971. Reprint of 1827 Edition) p.296.

5. Philips & Darlington, *Records of Mining and Metallurgy* 1857. Water pressure machines used high-pressure water as the source of energy. For further details with a list of Welsh applications, see Bick, Part 1, pp.40-47.

6. Bennett, J. (Ed). *Minera Lead Mines and Quarries* (Wrexham Maelor Borough Council, 1995), p.72 See also *M.J.* 1885, p.353.

7. P.R.O. BT31/2462/12579.

8. *M.J.* 1879, pp.510, 623.

9. Hunt, R. *British Mining* (1887) p.627.

10. As result of many accidents, manriding was generally forbidden, but in 1958 I tasted this harrowing mode of conveyance to the bottom of Berehaven Copper Mines, Co. Cork. At least it was quicker than ladders.

11. C. Le Neve Foster *Ore and Stone Mining*, (1897) pp.416-7.

12. For a general introduction, see - Burt *British Ore Preparation Techniques* (1982).

13. *M.J.* November 19th 1870.

14. C. Le Neve Foster *Ore and Stone Mining*, pp.576-7.

15. C. Le Neve Foster *Ore and Stone Mining*, pp.573-4.

16. *M.J.* 1881, p.131.

17. Nogara wrote a paper published in Sardinia on his Frongoch experiences, 'Descrizione della Miniera di Frongoch, Resoconti delle ruinioni dell' *Associozone Mineraria Sardo* Anno VI No.3, (1901). I have been unable to trace a copy in this country.

18. E.H. Davies *Machinery for Metalliferous Mines*, 2nd edn. 1902, pp.496/7.

19. Liquid starting resistances consisted of a large tank of electrolyte, (often salt-water which gave off chlorine gas) in which the distance between two poles could be varied by a lever. I witnessed such a contraption working at a Ffestining slate mine in 1962.

20. B.G.S. Report by John Mitchell, August 1903.

21. E.H. Davies, *Machinery for Metalliferous Mines* (1902), p.498.

22. For more on ponds and leats, see Bick, Part 6, pp.17-26.

PART 2 – INDUSTRIAL ARCHAEOLOGY

GENERAL DESCRIPTION

The continuous development of the site, culminating in the wholesale removal of much of the waste for re-processing, has left a very complicated palimpsest of remains. Most of the standing buildings are along the higher ground to the north-west of the dressing-floors, but from beneath the tipped rubble emerge walls and other structures, most of which can be identified.

Very little can now be recognised of the mine before the Taylors acquired it. There was an '*old engine shaft*', which presumably retained its name thereafter, and a pumping wheel (the location of which is uncertain) powered by water from at least two reservoirs.

The fifty years of working by the Taylors enlarged the workings very considerably, and most of the visible remains date from their period. Individual structures can be dated by reference to maps, to the known history, and occasionally by internal phasing within a building.

The earliest depiction appears to be the Tithe Award map of 1847. This shows the engine-house of 1841, a building to the south-west (perhaps next to Engine Shaft), the office with two smaller structures to the north-west, and another building further to the south-west in a plot described as '*Cae Gwaith Mwyn and Buildings*', which was listed as being under pasture. Above the buildings was a long leat, ending in a possible water-wheel near the Engine Shaft, and with a second branch ending just south-west of the engine-house.

Moissenet described the workings in great detail in 1860, and his plans are of considerable accuracy (see fig.17). He stated that two shafts were sunk below the 143 metres (78 fathom) level. On his plan, only Pryse's Shaft and Taylor's Shaft are indicated, both evidently productive since tramways ran from them to the dressing mills. The mills took advantage of the slope of the ground so that the spillway of one water-wheel either fed the next wheel in the sequence or provided water for the various buddles and separators.

By 1878 there had been considerable change again and the scale of this is apparent from the list of machinery in the inventory of that year (see p.45) and from the OS 25" map of 1885 which shows the enlarged dressing mills. It is equally clear, however, that many of the new buildings must have been insubstantial (like so many contemporary mine-buildings elsewhere), since by 1904 they had been removed and almost no trace now remains.

60 inch PUMPING ENGINEHOUSE

The most spectacular building remaining on the site, the enginehouse was built c.1870 to house a Cornish beam-engine with a 60" cylinder and 11 foot stroke built by the Sandicroft Foundry (Flintshire). The date of purchase is unknown, but it was probably soon after the opening of the railway to

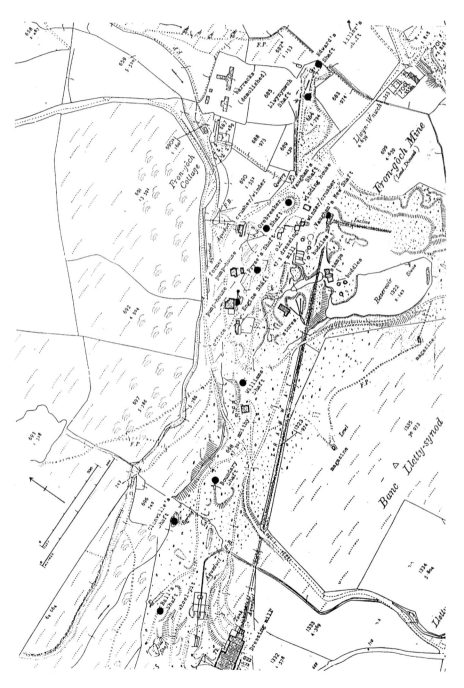

FIG. 10. General site plan, showing location of shafts. (R.C.A.H.M.W.).

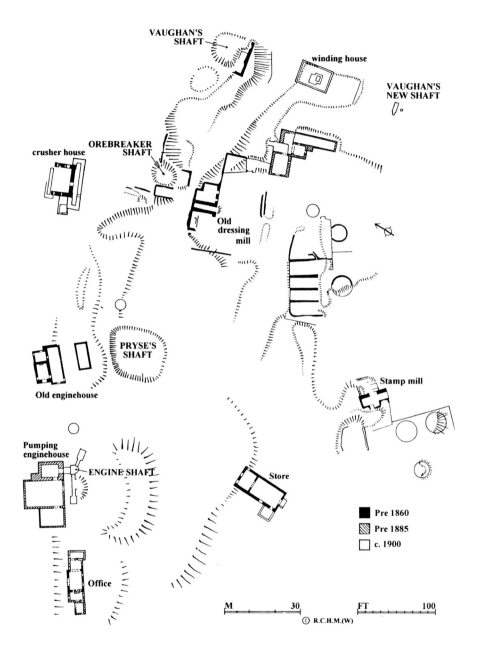

FIG. 11. General plan of the north-east area. (R.C.A.H.M.W.).

55

Trawscoed since, without the railway, neither cheap coal nor cheap bricks would have been readily available so far inland. The engine was probably dismantled after the sale of 1904, when it was described in the catalogue as having a double cast-iron beam and a 36 foot spear-rod. The eastern half of the enginehouse was demolished many years ago (Note the brick chimney has blown down since this chapter was written). Adjacent is the boiler house for the two 36 foot by seven foot Lancashire boilers, and a coal store. The pump-rod remains in the shaft. To either side is a balance-bob pit, that to the west being the original one. When the shaft was deepened and the weight of the pump-rods increased, a second pit, angled so as to clear the existing outlet culvert and to avoid weakening the foundations of the building, was devised.

Structurally the enginehouse is in several phases, although clearly it was designed as a single unit. The chimney is constructed of large blocks of rubble and, although the quoins are only dressed above roof-level, it is obvious that the rest of the building was added to it. Presumably the free-standing chimney was built first, then the rest of the enginehouse constructed around the engine itself. The south-east façade (the bob-wall) is faced with large rubble blocks more or less well dressed, clearly for effect. The top of the chimney is built in yellow brick. Beam-slots and the scar of a stair-way indicate the basic internal arrangements.

The boiler house was added, using altogether smaller rubble for the walls. The scar of its very peculiar hipped roof is still visible. Added again is the wall of the coal store, in the same sort of masonry as the boiler house.

25 inch STEAM WINDER & CRUSHER (south-east of the dressing mills) The only buildings surviving from the dressing-mill complex shown on the 1885 OS 25" map are the winding enginehouse of c.1870, the crusher house, and various attached buildings. The earliest part is the enginehouse, which is very similar in detail to the pumping-enginehouse. The bob-wall is built of long rubble blocks, the chimney is structurally free-standing, and the top of the chimney was of brick. This building held the 25" rotative engine, but it is not clear how the winding-gear operated, since no known shaft is in direct line with the engine, although it is roughly aligned with Vaughan's Shaft.

It is also not known how long the engine continued in use. It had been removed before the sale of 1904, but there are concrete blocks and hold-fast bolts in the fly-wheel pit suggesting that something was still operating there until at least the end of the century.

Attached to the enginehouse are two ruined buildings; one at the north-west now totally ruined but built of massive rubble blocks, and the other very long but with slighter walls. Originally both were under a deep sloping roof. One of them (probably the long building) must have been the boiler house.

56

FIG. 12. The 60 inch pumping enginehouse, c.1860
The engine came from Sandicroft foundary. (R.C.A.H.M.W.).

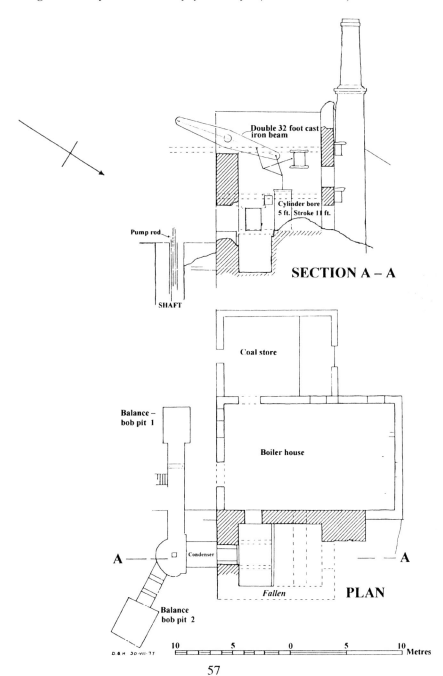

Double 32 foot cast iron beam

Pump rod

Cylinder bore 5 ft. Stroke 11 ft.

SHAFT

SECTION A – A

Coal store

Balance – bob pit 1

Boiler house

A

Condenser

A

Fallen

PLAN

Balance bob pit 2

D.B.H 30-VII-77

10   5   0   5   10 Metres

57

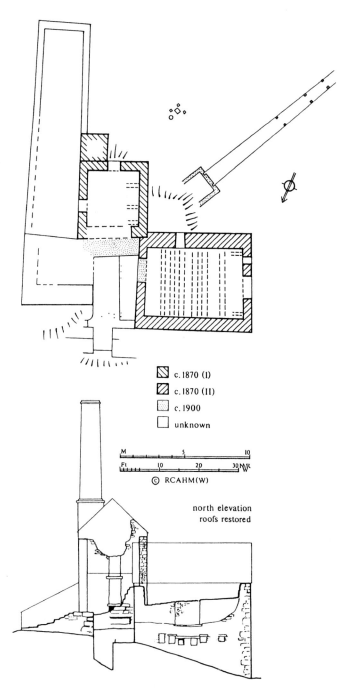

c.1870 (I)

c.1870 (II)

c.1900

unknown

© RCAHM(W)

north elevation
roofs restored

FIG. 13. The steam winder and crusher, c.1870. (R.C.A.H.M.W.).

58

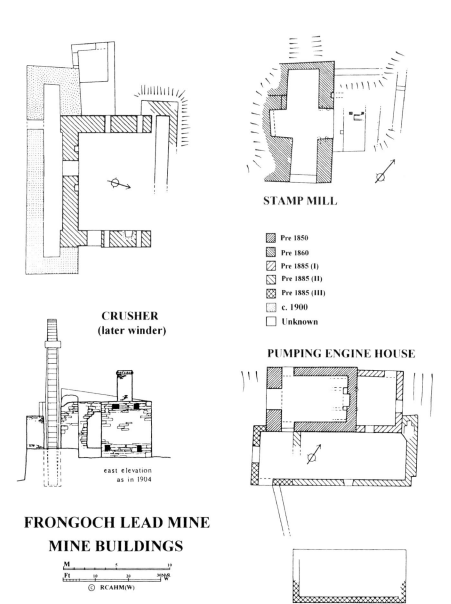

CRUSHER
(later winder)

STAMP MILL

▨	Pre 1850
▧	Pre 1860
▨	Pre 1885 (I)
▨	Pre 1885 (II)
▨	Pre 1885 (III)
☐	c. 1900
☐	Unknown

PUMPING ENGINE HOUSE

east elevation
as in 1904

FRONGOCH LEAD MINE
MINE BUILDINGS

M ────── 5 ────── 10
Ft ── 10 ── 20 ── 30
© RCAHM(W)

FIG. 14. Stamp Mill, Crusher/Winder and Enginehouse
for re-circulating water. (R.C.A.H.M.W.).

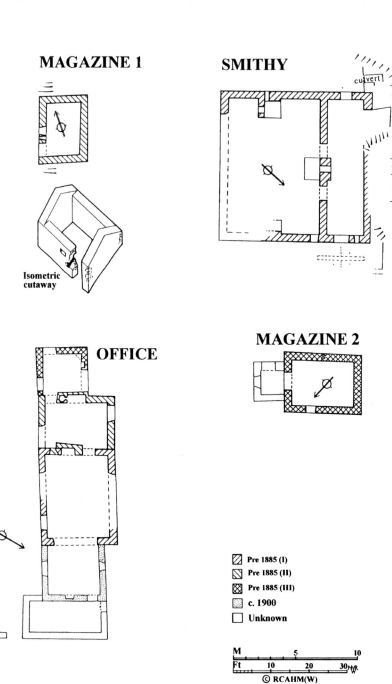

MAGAZINE 1

Isometric
cutaway

SMITHY

culvert

OFFICE

MAGAZINE 2

Pre 1885 (I)
Pre 1885 (II)
Pre 1885 (III)
c. 1900
Unknown

M   5   10
Ft   10   20   30
© RCAHM(W)

FIG. 15. Ancillary Buildings. (R.C.A.H.M.W.).

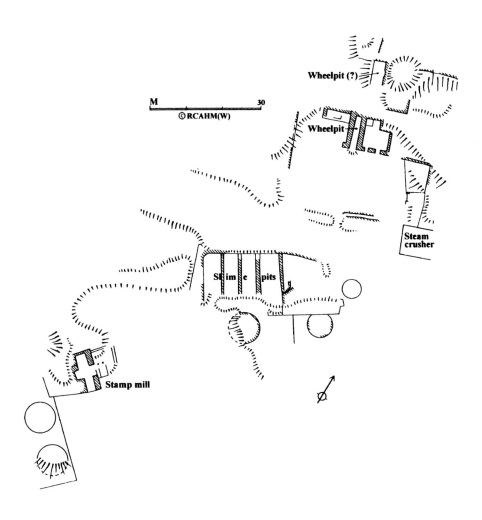

M   30

©RCAHM(W)

Wheelpit (?)

Wheelpit

Steam crusher

Slime pits

Stamp mill

FIG. 16. Dressing mills area, 1984. (R.C.A.H.M.W.).

61

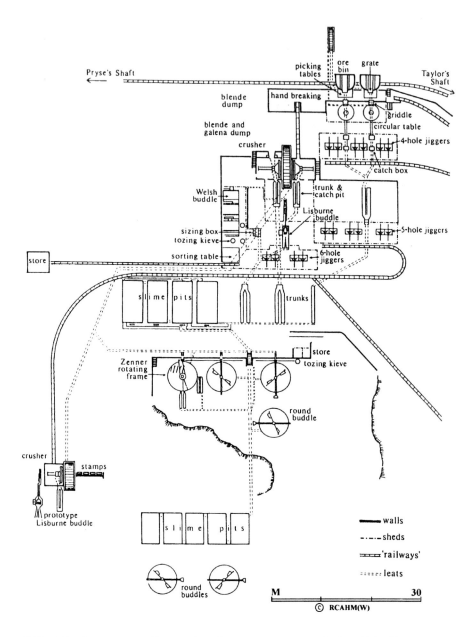

FIG. 17. Dressing mills, 1860 (after Moissenet). (R.C.A.H.M.W.).

To the south-west of the fly-wheel pit is the crusher house, built of rough rubble with large, roughly-squared quoins. It was originally gabled, and the north wall was partially rebuilt. The crusher rolls were supported on six massive cross-beams set deep into the walls. Subsequently a chute for crushed rock was contrived in the south wall, whence led a wooden channel of which the wooden and concrete supports survive.

40 inch PUMPING ENGINEHOUSE for recirculating water
In 1841 Taylor brought in a steam-engine with a 40" diameter cylinder. The water, which it pumped from an unspecified shaft, was recirculated over the water-wheels. This building, which is shown on the 1847 Tithe Award map, must have been its enginehouse. It is considerably ruined, but the massive bob-wall remains, faced with long blocks of rubble. In the north-east wall are the stumps of heavy beams. A secondary building attached to the south-east is probably the boiler-house, with perhaps a coal yard further to the south.

It is not certain whether the engine was rotative, pumping by flat rods from the present Engine Shaft, or whether it pumped directly from a now lost shaft immediately outside the enginehouse. However, no sign of such a shaft survives, either on the ground or on the plan of c.1870. Moreover, a rotative engine would have been the more useful since it could have been used for other purposes, such as crushing or winding, as well. But conversely there is no sign of the supports for the flywheel of a rotative engine or of the necessary angle-bob for the flat rods (since the enginehouse does not align with Engine Shaft). Also, the diameter of the cylinder is uncommonly large for a rotative engine and, in the advertisement of 1847, the engine is not described as rotative. Finally there is no reason why this isolated enginehouse (almost the only building on the site in 1841) should not have been aligned with Engine Shaft if flat rods were to have been used, and the Tithe Award map clearly shows a short watercourse, presumably for the pumped water, between the engine-house and the main leat.

The engine was sold in 1847. A flue and fireplace were inserted into the north-east wall of the enginehouse later, but there is no clue to the new function of the building. It is not mentioned by Moissenet, which suggests that it did not contain machinery at the time of his visit. (Note. The north-east corner was demolished some years ago - D.E.B.).

CRUSHER/WINDER
To the north-west of Orebreaker Shaft is a puzzling building of several phases, consisting of a much-altered crusher house, extant in 1885, with a second wheel-pit added. The crusher house has only three walls, with a contemporary wheel-pit across the open fourth side. The walls are built of massive blocks of squared rubble, with shallow *pilasters* at the corners. The original form of the roof is uncertain, since the tops of the walls have been lowered. Two sets of slots indicate the position of massive beams, and blocked openings in the south-east wall suggest that a basement storey has

been totally filled. It is possible that this was the location of the crusher driven by a 20 foot by three foot water-wheel in 1878. Moissenet does not mention it, so it may well be later than 1860. It has not proved possible to reconstruct it satisfactorily, but there is a similar crusher house at Glogfawr Mine.

By 1904 the building had been totally altered. A huge wheel-pit had been added against the south-east wall, and the crusher had been replaced by shafting and gearing for a belt-driven engine, winding from Orebreaker Shaft and driven off the 50 foot waterwheel visible on the photograph of c.1900. The new machinery is listed in detail in the sale catalogue. The roof had been altered: a small fireplace was inserted into the north-east wall and a chimney of small rubble masonry with a brick cap was added. At the same time, a small structure was attached to the south-west end of the building, containing the concrete base for an unidentified machine.

DRESSING MILLS
The location of the dressing mills in use before 1860 is uncertain. There was a water-powered crusher and jigger in 1841, possibly in the stamp mill building (q.v.), but nothing identifiable as a mill is shown on the Tithe Award map of 1847. Moissenet's plan shows that by 1860, however, there was an elaborate complex on three main levels, much of which can still be traced in outline (The site is now being buried in waste from adjacent sawmills - D.E.B.). The inventory of 1878 suggests that by then many of the water-wheels had been replaced, and by 1885 the mills had been almost totally rebuilt.

Moissenet's mills were divided into three main levels. The Upper Mill was just below a tramway between Pryse's Shaft and Taylor's Shaft and ore-bins by the tramway fed rock-breakers, classifiers and jiggers which were driven by a water-wheel close to the later Orebreaker Shaft. The walls of what may be this wheel-pit can be seen, with traces of the leat above it. The sorted rock passed to the crushing rolls in the Middle Mill and these were powered by a water-wheel of 29 feet 6 inches diameter. In the same building were two banks of jiggers and the Lisburne buddles. The upper revetment wall of the mill and the walls of the wheel-pit can be seen, although the sites of individual machines cannot be identified.

Below the Middle Mill was another tramway system, to the store, the stamp mill and the dumps and a possible fragmentary section of this can be seen west of the later steam-powered crusher house. Further to the south was the Lower Mill, where the enriched sands were allowed to settle in a series of slime pits and were then finally sorted in the round buddles. The four slime pits can be seen, and the outlines of two round buddles: one has been overlaid by the walls of a later structure, and there is another smaller one, presumably later, to the north east. A further series of slime pits and buddles shown to the south on Moissenet's plan has been destroyed.

The inventory of 1878 hints at expansion, listing '*six small waterwheels on the flooring*', together with '*Collieries Jiggers and Coal Rake*'. This strange machine could possibly be the Lisburne buddle, unknown outside the area and, therefore, not understood by the agent preparing the inventory. The steam-powered crusher was in use soon afterwards, if not then.

By 1885 the mills had been considerably enlarged, but the principles of operation were the same. The Upper Mill remained, with its isolated water-wheel and the tramway. The Middle Mill was substantially the same, but perhaps no longer with waterpowered crushers since the wheel-pit appears to be empty. However, the Lower Mill had been enlarged. To the north-east of the slime pits a long structure reaches as far as the crusher house. It was probably open-sided, since two buddles on the south east are partly covered. A further four buddles of various sizes (one an old one) stood further to the south east. The stamp-mill building survived, but possibly without a water-wheel. South of it were three buddles, two of which are still visible. Further to the south east, Moissenet's five slime pits and two buddles were increased to two sets of slime pits and three buddles.

By 1904 this had changed dramatically as all dressing was now undertaken at the new mill at Wemyss. Some of the buddles and slime pits remained, however, and a wheel in the Middle Mill (shown on the 1904 OS 25" map) suggests that the crusher here was still operational. The Wemyss mill (built in 1898), like the older mills, was built on a steep slope so that each successive machine was fed by gravity. A series of revetment walls and platforms supported the machinery, and the plans of the contemporary mill at Cwmystwyth (see E.H. Davies, *Machinery for Metalliferous Mines* (1902) figs.302-308) give an idea of the scale of such an integrated plant.

A final stage may be identified. A plan showing the lead and zinc dumps (undated, but post-1904) indicates the line of the aerial ropeway to Gwaith-goch. This began at the side of the steam-powered crusher, to which ran a pipeline from the north. There was also an incline to the dumps south of Vaughan's New Shaft. It would appear that the eastern end of the tramway to Wemyss had already been destroyed, although the western end, running under the road, is still in existence.

ANCILLARY BUILDINGS
1. The Office stands on a revetted platform and, of four constructional phases, all but one are shown on the 1885 OS 25" map. The earliest part was in use by 1847. This single, large, two-storey unit has walls of thin split, slatey, rubble masonry plastered inside and out. To it was added a two-storey room to the south west, which had fireplaces in the gable (with the ground-floor fireplace including a brick oven). Beyond this was another addition, single storeyed and with two small fireplaces in the west end. The final alteration, an addition at the north-east end, was built before 1904. It was also single storey, with segmental arches of yellow brick over the windows.

2. The Smithy was a large building with an undivided main room and a contemporary lean-to-rear section, already in use by 1878. The façade (now mostly demolished) was faced with long blocks of dressed rubble, and the rest of the walls were of smaller, rougher masonry. There were three hearths and the holes for the bellows can still be seen in two of them. The rear section probably contained shafting from the water-wheel which drove the bellows, and the general location of the wheel is indicated by holdfast bolts outside the building. Water-wheels for the smithy are listed both in the 1878 inventory and the 1904 sale catalogue. By the western corner of the building is a low vaulted culvert.

3. Magazines: two buildings are so named on the OS 25" maps. On structural grounds they seem to be of two different dates. Magazine 1 has walls of rubble masonry in lime mortar, and probably a slate floor. It had one very small window and between it and the doorway was a narrow, splayed chute through the wall. It is fairly close to a small trial level. Magazine 2 is slightly larger, and had an additional unit built after 1885 in the form of a large porch. It had a suspended wooden floor, and in the thickness of the wall are possible ventilation slots. It seems that it may have been a store for high explosive with a separate storage area for detonators.

4. The store (see general plan) is a long ruined building with walls of rubble masonry above a plinth of coursed masonry. At the south end is a loading platform. Footings at the south-west corner indicate the position of a small secondary building. The form of the roof is uncertain, but it may have been in two parts, gabled at the southern end and taller and hipped to the north. Moissenet's plan indicates a store in the right general location, but it was either much smaller (about four metres square) or conventionalised. The present building was in use by 1885.

THE SHAFTS
The remains of six shafts can still be seen. The locations of others can be pinpointed on maps, but no trace now remains.

1. Vaughan's Shaft (or Taylor's Shaft), shown on the 1885 OS 25" map. The southern wall of the shaft-head survives, with a recess for the balance bob of a pumping engine. A ladderway used to be visible.

2. Vaughan's New Shaft, replaced Vaughan's Shaft about 1880. It is blocked below a concrete lip. The bolts for the head-frame and the foundations of the enginehouse (both of which are shown on the photograph of c.1904) are still visible.

3. Orebreaker Shaft, blocked and with ruins of three sides of the shaft-head walling only. The name presumably derives from the proximity of the stone breakers in the dressing mill.

4. Engine Shaft, blocked but evidently still subsiding. The walls of the shaft and its associated balance-bob pits are built of good-quality rubble masonry.

5. Pryse's Shaft, although concealed by 1904, is probably located in a deep hollow in the spoil-tips south of the 1841 enginehouse.

6. Boundary Shaft (west of the modern road) is now full of dumped rubbish. A fine horse-whim circle is visible nearby.

At the Wemyss Mine, Ball's and Glanville's shafts can also be identified.

✿ ✿ ✿ ✿ ✿

PLATE XVII. Wemyss Mine and the big pumping wheel, from an old postcard. (N. Parkhouse).

PRODUCTION & EMPLOYMENT
1878 – 1903

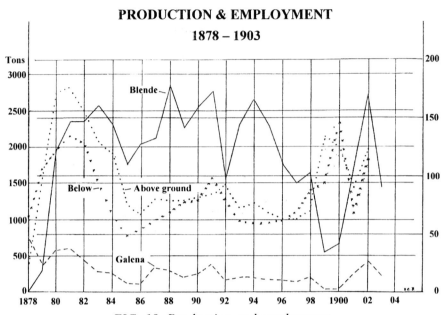

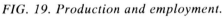

FIG. 19. Production and employment.

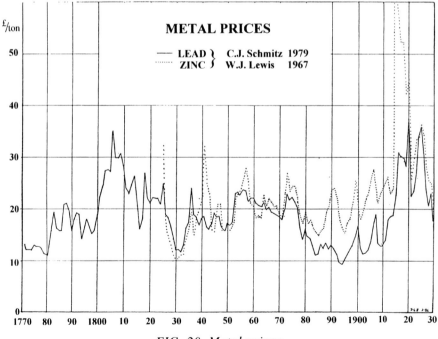

FIG. 20. Metal prices.

PART 3 – APPENDIXES

APPENDIX I

Principal Shafts on the Frongoch Lodes[*]
(From East to West)

Mine	Name of Shaft	Vertical or Inclined	Depth (Fathoms)
FRONGOCH	Miller's	V	24
	Edwards	I	78
	Llwynwnuch	I	24
	Taylor's (Vaughan's)	I	154
	Vaughan's New	V	90/154
	Orebreaker	I	66
	Pryse's	I	105
	Engine	V	117
	Williams'	V	66
	Boundary	V	56
WEMYSS	Glanville's	I	16
	Ball's	I	76
	Road	V	18
WEST FRONGOCH	Brook	I	30
GRAIGGOCH	Red Rock	I	23
	New	I	73

* Based on George Trefois, 'Notes on the Frongoch Mines', 1903 (BGS) with additions.

APPENDIX II

Frongoch Production Figures, to nearest ton.

Date	Lead Ore	Blende (Zinc Ore)	Date	Lead Ore	Blende (Zinc Ore)
Pre-1825	3000*	3000*	1864	1455	107
1825	4		1865	1540	
1826	24		1866	1560	
1827	2		1867	1586	
1828	1		1868	1170	
1829	64		1869	1500	
1830	216		1870	1248	
1831	158		1871	1314	60
1832	283		1872	1145	
1833	387		1873	1040	
1834	457		1874	850	
1835	807		1875	1162	
1836	892		1876	990+	
1837	671		1877	1070+	
1838	447		1878	749	
1839	78	5426 tons	1879	370	300
1840		ref O.T. Jones	1880	570	1965
1841			1881	600	2350
1842			1882	460	2350
1843			1883	285	2558
1844			1884	260	2304
1845	900*		1885	125	1750
1846	876+		1886	104	2050
1847	79+		1887	330	2110
1848	913+		1888	310	2850
1849	999+		1889	220	2260
1850	1854+		1890	250	2550
1851	1861+		1891	390	2762
1852	1772+		1892	155	1560
1853	1372+		1893	210	2321
1854	1232+		1894	205	2645
1855	1062+		1895	185	2305
1856	1442+		1896	165	1769
1857	1355+		1897	147	1509
1858	1037+		1898	201	1649
1859	1033	153	1899	43	549
1860	1110	52	1900	42	663
1861	1422	52	1901	333	1739
1862	1946		1902	426	2762
1863	1498	194	1903	202	1453
				58,295	49,701 tons

Notes:

Silver returned in the years 1859, 60, 62, 63, 75-81, 1896, 1901, 03. Total = 24,414 oz.

Post 1845, the above figures are extracted from Mineral Statistics, except in those years where Frongoch output was aggregated with other Lisburne mines.

For further details, see Burt, R. et al. *The Mines of Cardiganshire*, (Exeter: Department of Economic History, University of Exeter, 1985). The blende figures in particular are incomplete, the *Mineral Statistics* not listing this mineral pre-1854.

* = estimate;   + = *Money*, November 6th 1878.

1824-39, NLW Crosswood II, 1045, 1174.

Ores extracted from the dumps post - 1903 are additional.

APPENDIX III

Frongoch Ownership & Management (1860-1903)
(Abstracted from Roger Burt, *The Mines of Cardiganshire*, 1985)

OWNERSHIP

1860-67	John Taylor & Sons
1868-77	Lisburne Mining Co Ltd
1878-82	Frongoch Lead Mine Co Ltd
1883-85	Frongoch Mining Co Ltd
1886-89	John Kitto & Sons
1890-97	John Kitto
1898	Société Anonyme Minière
1899-1903	Société Anonyme Des Mines De Frongoch

MANAGEMENT

1862-3	Henry Thomas
1864-7	Thomas Ball
1868-77	John Taylor & Sons
1879-88	John Kitto & Son
1889-94	Abel Paull
1895-97	John Owen
1898	Max C Stegemann
1899	B. Nogara
1900-03	G.H. Trefois

SECRETARY

1872-4	Henry Taylor
1877	H.H. Oakes
1879-81	H.R. Moore

Other names included D. Simmons, R. Glanville, P. Garland and H. Clemes.

APPENDIX IV

LÉON MOISSENET'S VISIT TO FRONGÔCH IN 1860

by

Stephen Briggs*

Introduction

The purpose of the writer's original contribution to this monograph, when printed in 1986, was to draw attention to the existence of important mid-19th century observations on British metalliferous mines, particularly those published in Paris by the remarkable French engineer Léon-Vivant Moissenet (1831-1906), in the hope of encouraging others to examine his and other early foreign travellers' accounts. Whilst at that time considerable effort was made both to offer a general overview and provide useful details about lead processing at the Lisburne Mines, because of the nature of that publication, translation was abbreviated to cover only a fraction of the original account. Since that shorter piece is retained here, readers keen to access Moissenet's observations in greater detail are referred to his original published paper.

During the last ten years, a welcome number of useful studies and reprints have appeared in this field of industrial history. These include edited translations of a metallurgical tour to Britain by Dufrénoy, Élie de Beaumont, Coste and Perdonnet (Martell and Gill 1989;1990), and one tour by Moissenet himself (Martell and Gill 1992). From these and others already in print, it is clear that the value of such sources is now fully appreciated by historical metallurgists.

Subsequent to the publication of the original Frongôch monograph, the writer briefly visited the library of the École des Mines in Paris, seeking more detail of Moissenet's industry, and hoping to discover whether or not any worthwhile manuscript testimony survived to his travels, or to those of any other early mining engineers.

The library possesses a limited amount of material in Moissenet's hand, including a travel diary to Wales in 1855. His honours certificates are also accessible, together with some brief funding requests and reports on a number of journeys abroad. But Moissenet's were not the only accounts. The library holds a register of its pupils' theses testifying to an apparent requirement for taking study tours at home or abroad as part of their courses. The writer's limited time and access meant that he was able to see only a representative group of 19th century diaries and notebooks, some then only recently rescued from a damp basement to be conserved.

French student engineers browsed or even penetrated a number of British extractive and processing industries, including those of coal, iron, copper and lead, as well as railways and some heavy engineering works. From the

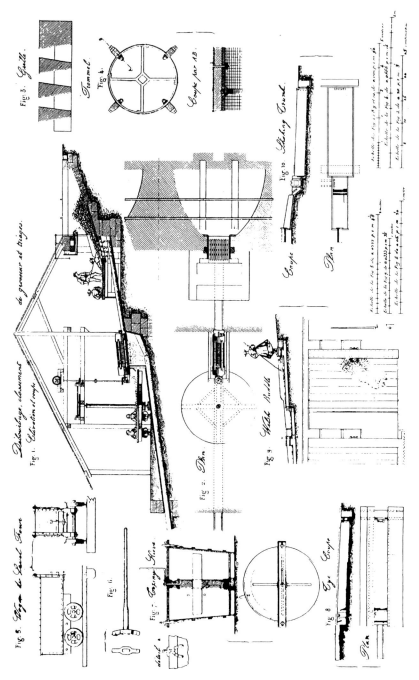

FIG. 21. Section from Moissenet's work.

73

nature of the material collected, it seems unlikely that they either thought of themselves as industrial spies, or, more significantly, they were received with any particular hostility by the industrialists they visited. The generous way in which some (very fragile) original Welsh engineers' coal pithead plans are bound up in at least one travel journal might also indicate a somewhat cavalier attitude to copyright on the parts of some British inventors or by the engineers who executed their plans.

Although, so far, there is no original manuscript account of Moissenet's Frongôch visit, from the evidence of his peers' diaries, it seems reasonable to conjecture that he probably had access to contemporary plans of the Lisburne Mines. Also, to judge from the remarkably high quality of production data he garnered, he was given the freedom of the Lisburnes' ledgers.

Presenting Moissenet (whose working life was spent almost entirely in the service of the École des Mines in Paris) ten years ago, the writer was inclined to consider Moissenet's contribution to metal extractive studies ostensibly in terms of traditions of French industrial espionage (Harris 1989). Espionage had indubitably existed among developing European economies from the 17th and 18th centuries, such practices tending to be attenuated, if not altogether terminated, by travel restrictions resulting from the Revolutionary and Napoleonic Wars.

The question of why Frenchmen chose to explore Britain after the Wars during the period 1815-30 was addressed by Ethel Jones in her doctoral dissertation over sixty years ago (Jones 1930). Although her attention best serves literary and artistic topics, she did recognise the important contribution engineers had made in the round to contemporary British topographical studies (pp.135-45). In particular, she noted a publishing interest in the developing British coal-waggon and railways, taken by Gallois who had visited from the School of Mines in 1818 (Jones 1930, 138-9).

Contrary to the present writer's thesis presented in 1986, in principle at least, Moissenet was actually following in the footsteps of a number of distinguished pupil or qualified engineers or gentlemen scholars keen to get to grips with British industrialisation. It is unclear why Moissenet should have set his mind upon such a comprehensive study of non-ferrous mining, but his publications do offer disinterested testimony to several important aspects of the industry not otherwise chronicled in contemporary English language publications.

Taking advantage of generous government bursaries, in 1857, 1858 and 1860 Moissenet embarked upon three tours to Britain, probably seeing Flintshire in 1858, and concentrating upon the Lisburne Mines in 1860 (Note 1). On tour he suffered two accidents, one involving a vehicle outside Caernarfon in 1860, and the other, which almost cost him his life, in 1866 at the Man Engine of Devon Great Consols Mine.

In later life, he became consulting engineer to the Montébras tin mine, Creuse, where he was to put to use his foreign observations. Among other innovations there, he introduced the Lisburne Buddle.

Moissenet enjoyed correspondence and friendship with several noted mining engineers, his interest and advice being recognised to the advantage of local mining captains all over Britain, and particularly in Cornwall (Micaud 1909). However, the greatest testimony to his endeavours are his publications in the *Annales des Mines*, printed during and soon after his British travels. These include accounts of lead mining in Flintshire (1857), lead smelting in Shropshire (1862; Martell and Gill 1992), and aspects of mining in Cornwall and Devon (Moissenet 1858, 1862). The paper which concerns us here, however, is his 1866 treatise on lead mining in Cardiganshire.

THE 1866 MEMOIR ON THE LISBURNE MINES*

* In summarising, and to a lesser degree, in editing this work, references to the original text are within square brackets thus:[], whilst editorial comment and reference to facts presented elsewhere in this monograph is bracketed thus:( ).

Entitled *"Préparation Mecanique du Minerai de Plomb aux Mines de Lisburne, Cardiganshire, Pays de Galles"* [On the mechanical preparation of lead ores at the Lisburne Mines, Cardiganshire, Wales], Moissenet's paper appeared in the *Annales de Mines*, Sér.6, tome ix, 1866, pp.1-137, after he had for the years 1862-5 given lectures at the School of Mines on the mechanical preparation of ores in Britain. The paper was accompanied by three plates of line drawings conveying his message in a clearer manner than perhaps it was possible to do verbally. Their contents were:-

Plate I – Fig.1, plan of Level Fawr, Pontrhydygroes, 1860; Fig.2, plan of Frongôch, 1860; Fig.3, Accessories of the Round Buddle; Fig.4, plan of same; Figs.5-11 sections and elevations of same.

Plate II.(concerns washing and grading of ores) – Fig.1, section of process house; Fig.2, plan of same; Fig.3, section of cast grate; Fig.4, trommel; Fig.5, Waggon at Level Fawr; Fig.6, [?]; Fig.7, tozing kieve; Fig.8, Tye, section of; Fig.9, plan and section of Welsh Buddle; Fig.10, plan and section of shaking trunk.

Plate III. Devoted entirely to 18 Figs, of plans and sections of the Lisburne Buddle.

Plate 1, Fig.2 has been re-drawn by A.J.Parkinson, and is printed above (Fig.17). It should be used in conjunction with Chapters 2 and 3 below. Plate III is omitted altogether, since it is of specialist interest, and could only be successfully reproduced with a near-full translation of its accompanying text. However, Plate II is reproduced here, and should be consulted in conjunction with the descriptive text (Fig.21).

The memoir shows that Moissenet was not only familiar with Frongôch and Level Fawr, but had also visited and studied Logaulas [Logylas], Glogfach, Esgair Mwyn and Grogwynion. However, some of it is concerned with more general aspects of the contemporary British lead industry and clearly, it is not possible to provide a complete translation of the paper here.

In collecting the most detailed information, he seems to have had a four-fold objective. This was first [chapter 1, pp.1-15], to relate the mines to local geology and mineralogy, making general observations upon how they were staffed, how many adits had been driven, and how the workshops could be related to the mines; secondly [chapter 2], to explain the methods employed in ore preparation, first at Level Fawr [pp.15-50], then at Frongôch [pp.51-77]; thirdly [chapter 3, pp.78-120], to provide a most detailed description of the contruction of the machinery contemporarily employed in ore processing at the Lisburne mines, offering a critical evaluation of their relative operative efficiencies; and, finally [chapter 4, pp.115-137], to examine the financial basis of the Lisburne Mines Company.

Several problems are to be encountered in summarising his work in English. The Mining Company's accounts books were no doubt kept in £. s. d. This, he converted to French francs at [15 shillings = 18 frs 75 centimes] or 25 frs to the £ sterling, and throughout, naturally enough, unit costs are given in francs. A similar difficulty is to be met with in his spatial measurements, where feet and inches are liberally interdigitated. Throughout his work the English fathom of six feet seems to equate with the old French toise of 6½ feet without the necessary adjustment. Equally, it is rarely clear when the English ton is being converted directly to the metric tonne of 1.0161 tons. Not unusually, he also refers throughout to '*Angleterre*' when Britain is certainly intended.

It is clear that contemporary and later writers on British mining were well acquainted with Moissenet's work, and, although a proper evaluation of his contribution to mining and metallurgical studies must await more detailed future study, it is worth noting that Hunt's *British Mining* of 1887 actually used the illustration of the Frongôch ore preparation shed presented here (Moissenet 1866, Pl.2; R. Hunt, 1887, per Burt 1982, Fig.1, p.15).

More recently, Palmer and Neaverson (1991a and b) have quoted from Moissenet's paper, though apparently unaware of the present writer's biographical note of 1986 (Note 2).

In the summary which follows, some effort is made to restrict discussion to Frongôch, but, as Frongôch and Level Fawr both belonged to the Lisburne Mines and as, particularly for economic considerations, Moissenet on

76

occasion treats both together, it has not always been found possible to exclude other mines from the summary.

1: DESCRIPTION OF LOCALITIES AND OUTCROPS
In his opening remarks, Moissenet immediately draws attention to the potential ascendancy of Frongôch over Level Fawr on account of the recent introduction of the Lisburne Buddle [pp.3-4], setting the general tenor of an argument about buddles and buddle efficiency which underlies the entire paper.

The main working at Frongôch was 1200 metres long, with veins of from 30-50 fms in length and from 10 to 30 ft thick, dipping to the west. These were oriented 8-12° E of true north. Branches at 2½° and 7½° west of north gave a 56 fm level east of Taylor's Shaft. There were two varieties of ore. One was laminated, the other fine-grained, with, more rarely, metallic lead. They yielded five ounces of silver per ton, and about one-eighth of the mineral extracted was of blende [p.10].

Mining was undertaken at four levels, four shafts being sunk below 78 fms, though only drained by adit to 24 fms. The levels were at 34, 44, 56, 66 and 78 fms. Little wood was used, since the country rock was very solid [p.11]. Running costs for driving the adits were about £3 10s 0d per metre through vein-ore, and about £3 0s 0d per metre for galleries and stopes. These costs were a little higher than those at Logylas, but considerably greater than those at Glogfach, where vein driving came to well under £2 0s 0d per metre.

As surface water was scarce at Frongôch, it was re-utilised for hydraulic power. Coal could be had for 25 shillings per tonne and about 100-120 tons was imported annually from Ruabon. The waterwheel of 60 h.p., 55 ft by 4 ft 6 ins (16.76 x 1.37 metres), which is described as having been served by vast reservoirs [p.12], was probably the large wheel at the Wemyss Pumping Station, to the west of the Frongôch complex. [The large wheelpit attached to the crushing mill here (see above p.59) was never as large as this, so far as is known, and in any case was built post-1883.]

The mine was served by mining captains from Cornwall and by local labourers who inhabited a line of terraced houses next to the mine [which are long since demolished]. Though not generally as skilled as the best of the Cornish elite, they were thought to be steady, hard-working and content with a moderate wage. Remuneration for underground workers fell under two distinct contract systems. 'Tutworkmen' were paid for piecework in shifting rock, while 'tributors' were paid according to the tonnage of concentrated ore sold. Frongôch was exploited entirely in the former way, and the introduction of the latter system at Logylas had brought about important changes. At this time [because veins were rich], tribute workers took home more than the others.

In 1859 there were 324 underground workers in the Lisburne Mines. They were paid a total of £11,933 1s 8d [298,328 frs] per annum, which represented some 53.92% of total overheads, (and gave each worker an average £36 16s 0d per annum). For both contract groups, the mining company provided powder, rope, candles and tools at a heavy subsidy, which in 1859 amounted to 7.55% of overheads. However, the greater 'perks' went to the 'tribute' workers [p.13].

Frongôch and Level Fawr dressing floors each employed 70-80. A few were men, some were boys and girls, but most were older women. Men were paid monthly and according to their ability, while the youngsters were paid by the day at between 4 and 11d., their average being 7d. The combined total cost of surface workers' pay at both mines in 1859 was £1,669 18s 0d. In that year 26,550 tonnes (metric) of ore left the mines for sale, and this included 2,454 tonnes of galena and 112 tonnes of blende [p.14].

In the main, Moissenet felt that working conditions at Frongôch were almost ideal. The company was fortunate to have waterpower, a content workforce and fair wages. But he expressed surprise that the owners of the mineral rights extracted such huge royalties, amounting here to 1/10th of the value of that which lay at the mine [pp.14-15].

2: THE SURFACE WORKINGS; ORE PREPARATION

Moissenet begins this section by explaining that the processes dealt with an ore that was poor in lead and strongly mixed with blende in an extremely hard quartzose gangue. Its yield was less than 6% of the extracted rock. As has been shown, (above pp.34,41 and Fig.7), in 1860 the mill was at four levels, set into a gentle slope, with the upper, middle and lower still in use. The fourth, lower still, was inactive at the time of the visit.

On the upper level ore sorting was organised as at Level Fawr, though the ore here passed through a grille with 1½ inches between the iron bars and a one-inch square mesh on the griddle [*trommel*]. At Level Fawr the mesh was smaller. The sorting operation was overseen by a lad with a long iron pick [*crochet* pp.17,51]. There were three groups of jiggers [*cribles*], with 6 four-holed, 6 five-holed and 4 six-holed, and two types of hand-jigger, one set of which had 7 perforations per inch. These were the only ones made of wire-mesh. There were also copper sieves, or sieves with copper bottoms, with a 1 mm mesh, which were used to finish washing the fine ore grains. Different types of griddle were used, with varied sizes and numbers of holes.

The Welsh buddles were inactive at the time of Moissenet's visit, and there was no shaking trunk. Instead, their place was taken by the Lisburne buddle and the sizing box.

The Lisburne buddle had first been built lower down in 1855 and its introduction had profoundly changed operations at the mine. It was essentially an inclined table, irrigated from the upper end by water, through which the ore was pushed diagonally by a heavy rake [*rateau*] with 21 teeth reverberating at 20 oscillations per minute. The resultant sorted ore was then shovelled into the topmost of four boxes, the smaller material falling into the other three, with only mud going through to the lowest box.

The sizing box [*classeur à jet d'eau*] consisted of three graded boxes through which water jets were directed from below [p.54]. The larger grains were resisted by the current, and fell into the first box, while the finer grains fell more slowly into a second box, and the mud escaped elsewhere. The machine was not working as efficiently as it might have been. Moissenet felt this was partly because of the way in which that particular model had been constructed, and partly because of its being forced to take a larger, more unsuitable grain size.

On the lower floors were three round buddles, a kieve with a mechanical agitator, and a rotating table. The latter, of German origin, was known as a Zenner rotating frame, and was used alongside the round buddles. Moissenet observed that its use here was nothing less than characteristic [p.53].

He then went on to explain in great detail the layout of the workings, as illustrated on his sketch plan [Plate 1] (see Fig.17 above), providing detailed measurements of each individual installation [pp.53-56]. The slime and finings issued at the lower end of the workings, after having passed through a grinder, the first Lisburne buddle, a crusher, five large slime pits and two round buddles. It cost £5 to wash each ton of ore.

In 1860 there were seven working waterwheels at Frongôch. Six were bucket wheels and the other had plain paddles. All were breast wheels. They ranged in size from 30 by 3 feet, through 18 by 9, 11 by 2, 6 by 1, to 5 by 1 feet [p.57].

Some attention was paid to the various qualities of mineral debris coming from each particular piece of plant, together with an account of its passage to the next machine [pp.58-63]. There then follows a much more detailed description of the Lisburne buddle, in which Moissenet enters into a closely reasoned account of its theoretical aims, its performance, its products, and the nature and function of its attendant plant. Its analyst concluded that, even used judiciously, this type of buddle was not to be recommended for use with a good number of ore-types [pp.64-72].

Tables follow, summarising the passage of ore around the workshops and the degree to which metal-enriched material was eventually deposited to be collected for despatch [pp. 74-77].

3: DESCRIPTION OF THE MACHINERY   See Plate II (here Fig.21)
Moissenet next details the dimensions, functions and products of the other machines, which were the slide [*trémie*], the grate [*grille en fonte*], and the

79

griddle [*trommel*]. Here [p.80] he adds the interesting detail, in a footnote, that the steel-gridded mesh sheets which made the casing on the griddle cylinders, were to be bought in Aberystwyth for 1s 6d per square foot. Those at Level Fawr only lasted two months. In using perforated sheet steel, rather than steel wire, the cylinders lasted six months. He goes on to provide unusual detail about the staff employed at the sorting tables of the grading shed. There were one strong small boy by the grille, four strong girls as sorters, standing two each side of the table and holding stretchers in their arms, and four more small girls, standing around the lower rotating table [p.82]. The big girls and the boy were each paid 9d per day and the younger girls got 5d. They dealt with 80 tonnes of ore per working day of 10 hours, while the mine produced an average of 65 tonnes per day.

Again, but only in a footnote, we are told great detail of the underground tram waggons, which ran on 2' 6" iron rails at 36 lbs weight per yard. The trams weighed 8 cwts unladen and at Logaulas would carry up to 0.9 tonne of mineral. The enterprise cost 5d per waggon load [p.83].

The dimensions of the driving rollers in the crushers are given [pp.84-5], and also details of the passage of water through the crushing gear and thence to the various canals [pp.86-8]. The largest waterwheel turned eight to nine revolutions per minute and its crusher processed 30-35 tonnes per day of 10 hours [p.85].

The jiggers are similarly treated by Moissenet, with statistics on the price of copper sheet, plain and unperforated, since 1844. Interestingly, for 1^1/8th" gauge it rose from 3s 2d to 6s 2d per square foot during the observed 15 year period. There is an account of the way in which the finings are dealt with by girl workers, who, for 9d per 10 hour day processed 6 tonnes of it [pp.90-91].

The shaking trunk, the tye, the Welsh buddle and the Lisburne buddle are again explained [91-94]. According to Moissenet, the Lisburne buddle was invented and first built at Frongôch by Captain Vigus late in 1855. Attention is drawn to the account of the buddle given by Philips and Darlington in their *Mining Records*, p.127. Moissenet goes to town on its construction and dimensions, working, hydraulic needs, motive force and unit costs. Here we find that its operation required 67 gallons of water per minute, and once more required four strong girls. It could process between 15 and 40 tonnes a day, and averaged 25. Up to 70% lead could be recovered from the first box on the buddle, 40% from the second, 25% from the third and 4% from the fourth [pp.95-106]. Moissenet next enters into a lengthy and complicated theoretical essay into the trajectories of mineral grains and their behaviour in the buddle [pp.107-114]. This, in turn, is followed by a similar analysis of the sizing box [pp.114-5].

After mentioning the (by then almost obsolete) crushing plant at Level Fawr, Moissenet next describes round buddles. They had been known for over 20 years, but had more recently fallen into disrepute on the continent. As they worked perfectly at the Lisburne Mines, however, a clear explanation of how they could be used to best advantage seemed to be needed. Basically, he explains that it had needed modifying to make it more successful [pp.116-20].

Finally, he explains the tozing kieve, which by that time was redundant at Frongôch, but was still in use at Level Fawr.

4: ECONOMIC ASPECTS

The Lisburne Mines were held as 400 shares of capital, each of £18 15s 0d, with a total invested capital of £7,500. By November 1864, the mines were worth £40,000, having produced a dividend of £403,500, with a capital value of only £90,000, the equivalent of 2,815% on original investment. About £500,000' worth of ore had probably been sold.

Total production figures for the Lisburne Mines group were given for the years 1857,8 and 9 showing net annual profits [taken from table 7, p.122, cf table 8, p.126]

Ore sold (tonne of 1000 kgs)	1857	1858	1859	total
galena	2,318.531	2,444.044	2,453.921	7,246.544
blende	278.706	153.033	541.285	541.285
market value (£)	34,523.30	32,985.80	34,489.90	101,207
less royalties	3,324.50	3,168.95	3,282.85	97,242.80
value to company	31,196.40	29,824.95	31,167.05	92,118.40
total expenditure	23,531.75	22,439.55	2,129.80	68,101.10
total net profit	7,664.65	7,385.40	9,037.25	24,889.75

The exploitation of galena and blende were intimately connected. From an average ton of galena at £13 18s 0d per ton, about £3 7s 0d or 24.11% was profit. Wages accounted for 9.66% and overheads 65.93% of the total returns. These compared well with the figures given by Phillips and Darlington in their *Records of Mining and Metallurgy*, p.255.

Interestingly, once it had arrived at the port of Aberystwyth, the purchaser of the ore paid its carriage. The cost varied from four to seven shillings per tonne, depending on its destination.

The ore was sold by the ton of 21 cwt [*quintaine*] of dry dressed mineral [*mineral sec*] amounting to 2,352 lbs. But weighing out at the mine was in 20 hundredweights of 119 lbs, grossing 2,380 lbs per ton. 2,380 - 2,352 lbs left an excess of 28 lbs, intended to cover any loss incurred in transport. The ore was carried in heavy-duty sacks by road to Aberystwyth, where it was assayed for humidity before embarkation. Hygroscopic readings of at least 2.45% water by weight were to be expected. Freight charges were estimated by wet weight, though marine tonnage was calculated upon dry. Aberystwyth Harbour Authority levied one shilling per ton carried [p.124].

A table follows, giving detailed monthly out-goings at both Level Fawr and Frongôch, together with average prices and wages. For Frongôch these annual figures run as follows:-

SALES

	1857 tons cwt qr	1858 tons cwt qr	1859 tons cwt qr
galena	2124 3 0	16,193 0 0	18,907 0 0
sold	1356 3 3	1,078 20 0	1,033 5 0
	(yield 6.38%)	(yield 6.53%)	(yield 5.46%)

price per 21 cwt ton

	£ s d	£ s d	£ s d
	15 8 3½	14 2 9¼	14 12 5

	tons cwt qr	tons cwt qr	tons cwt qr
blende	264 7 1	143 11 0	105 10 0
	£ s d	£ s d	£ s d
sold at	3 8 3¼	3 14 8	214 9 0

PRODUCTION COSTS:-

	£ s d	£ s d	£ s d
galena crop	0 11 2¼	0 9 3	0 14 0½
slimes	21 3 8	3 6 1½	3 8 7½
blende, crop	0 10 0	10 0 0	

It is difficult to analyse the monthly averages provided on the same table, since these include complex factors relating to the other mines in the Lisburne complex (Glôgfach and Logaulas) which processed at Level Fawr. Moissenet offers several useful observations upon these collected data. Between 1857 and 1859, production at Level Fawr rose while that at Frongôch fell. Until 1857, Frongôch had upheld the production of the group as a whole, then, after tribute payments had been introduced at Logaulas in 1857, their roles had virtually reversed. The relative profits per ton (21 cwts) for these years were:-

	1857 £ s d	1858 £ s d	1859 £ s d
Level Fawr	14 2	3 2 2	4 18 3
Frongôch	5 9 0	2 12 10	2 11 3

Profits at Level Fawr had risen from 4.43% to 14.26%. Percentage yields at Frongôch declined slightly from 6.58 and 6.55, to 5.46%, but these differences were to be put down to the extreme difficulty with which ore-washing was undertaken, owing largely to the presence of blende. The production of both crop and slimes thus rose appreciably over the three-year period [p.129]. But, whilst the cost of raising a ton of ore at Frongôch was cheaper than at Level Fawr, it came to only 5½d at the former and 1s 6½d at the latter and processing inflated these figures to 12s and 16s respectively.

A discussion follows detailing relative production costs of crops, slimes and halvans from all the Lisburne mines.

Moissenet was anxious to establish the exact yield of metal from the ore, but in this he did succeed. Although somewhat affected by the blende within the ore, lead crop from Frongôch, like that from Level Fawr, was probably up to 78% and around 55% from the fines.

He discusses at length the way in which losses of mineral were part of the manufacturing process [pp.134-5], and offers the theoretical mean of 9% loss at Frongôch [p.136].

In a critical summary of his work at the Lisburne Mines, Moissenet regretted that hand cobbing by hammer had disappeared. Frongôch was all but a model workshop, though sizing griddles should be introduced, and these would complement the virtues of the Lisburne buddle. *"Thus complete, it seems to me that ore processing at Frongôch, already close to a working perfection, would in future rank among those classic establishments which served as milestones to progress in the art of mining"* [p.137].

Notes

1.   *contra* Palmer and Neaverson (1989a, p.23; 1989b, pp.318-19), who erroneously suggest that Moissenet visited Frongôch in 1864-5. Manuscripts at the *École de Mines* show that during 1863-4 the Frenchman requested authority to offer a course of lectures on ore-processing at the Lisburne Mines. According to a lengthy footnote prefatory to his printed paper, the Minister of Public Works granted him permission. Consequently, Moissenet lectured on the subject in 1864-5 (when he apparently did not travel). Elsewhere, however, Palmer and Neaverson (1989b,322) note that his visit to Frongôch was in 1860, though it is difficult to find in his account the text they ascribe to Moissenet's page 61.

2.   Curiously, Palmer and Neaverson's *Review* paper gives no page references defining the parameters of Moissenet's work, although their contribution to the *Bulletin of the Peak Mines Historical Society* does (1989b, p.342; this paper also cites the *British Mining* No.30 (1986), though not obviously in the context of Moissenet). Furthermore, the *Review* quotation it ascribes to Moissenent's pen (in translation 1989a, p.23) is twice attributed to his page 22, when it actually appears on page 21. Moissenet accurately subheaded this piece, *Welsh Buddle or Flat Buddle*, a title oddly contorted to translate Wash-kiln by Hunt in his publication (1884, p.90), an important terminological difference of more than passing historiographic interest curiously not thought worthy of comment by Palmer and Neaverson in 1989.

ACKNOWLEDGEMENT

The writer thanks Mme Marie-Noelle Maisonneuve, librarian and archivist to the *École des Mines*, Paris, and also her colleagues for cooperation and generous help in his search for information about French Mining Engineers. David Bick, Richard Bird, Michael Gill, Brian Malaws and Tony Parkinson have all kindly assisted in different ways. The views expressed and any errors of fact remain entirely the writer's responsibility.

*Current Address: Llwyn Deiniol, Llanddeiniol, Llanrhystud,
Dyfed SY23 5DT.

REFERENCES

Burt, R. *A Short History of British Ore Preparation Techniques in the Eighteenth and Nineteenth Centuries* (Aalst-Waalre, Holland: 1982).

Harris, J.R. "French Industrial Espionage in Britain in the Late Eighteenth Century" *Journal of the Royal Society of Arts* (1989), pp.629-634.

Hunt, R. *British Mining*, 1887

Jones, E. *Les Voyageurs Français en Angleterre de 1815 à 1830* (Paris: Boccard, 1930).

Martell, H.M. and Gill, M.C. "Voyage Métallurgique en Angleterre" *Bulletin of the Peak District Mines Historical Society*, Vol.10 (1989), pp.253-265.

Martell, H.M. and Gill, M.C. "Ore-Hearth Smelting (Voyage Métallurgique en Angleterre)" *British Mining*, No.41 (1990), pp.22-36.

Martell, H.M. and Gill, M.C. "Lead Smelting in Welsh Furnaces at Pontesford, Shropshire" *Bulletin of the Peak District Mines Historical Society*, Vol.11 No.6 (1992), pp.287-312 [A translation of Moissenet's paper.]

Micaud, J. "Notice sur Léon Moissenet, Inspecteur Général des Mines" *Annales des Mines*, Sér.7, tome XV (1909), pp.490-508.

Moissenet, L.V. "Mémoire sur le gisement de Minerai de Plomb dans la calcaire Carbonifère du Flintshire" *Annales des Mines*, Sér.5 tome XI (1857), pp.351-446.

Moissenet, L.V. "Description du procèdé Anglais pour les essais de cuivre par la voie sèche" *Annales des Mines*, Sér.5 tome XIII (1858), pp.185-208.

Moissenet, L.V. "Excursion dans le Cornwall en 1857. Préparation mécanique du minerai d'étain" *Annales des Mines*, Sér.5 tome XIV (1859), pp.77-276.

Moissenet, L.V. "Les Usines à Plomb de Pontesford, près Shrewsbury (Shropshire). Traitement de la galène au Four Gallois" *Annales des Mines*, Sér.6 tome I (1861a), pp.445-484.

Moissenet, L.V. "Sur la fabrication du Minium à L'usine de Shrewsbury" *Annales des Mines*, Sér.6 tome I (1861b), pp.595-600.

Moissenet, L.V. "De l'éxtraction dans les mines de Cornwall. Puits inclinés et coudés" *Annales des Mines*, Sér.6 tome II (1862), pp.155-272.

Moissenet, L.V. "Préparation Mecanique du Minerai de Plomb aux Mines de Lisburne, Cardiganshire" *Annales des Mines*, Sér.6 tome IX (1866), pp.1-137.

Palmer, M. & Neaverson, P. "Nineteenth Century Tin and Lead Dressing: A Comparative Study of the Field Evidence" *Industrial Archaeology Review*, Vol.12 No.1 (1989a), pp.20-39.

Palmer, M. & Neaverson, P. "The Comparative Archaeology of Tin and Lead Dressing Floors in Britain during the Nineteenth Century" *Bulletin of the Peak District Mines Historical Society*, Vol.10 No.6 (1989b), pp.316-353.

APPENDIX V

EXPLORING FRONGOCH ADIT

by

Roy Fellows

The adit begins above the road at the west end of Wemyss mine and, after a good spell of dry weather, can still be explored as far as Engine Shaft by those sufficiently equipped and determined. We are indebted to Roy Fellows for the following account of his trips in the spring of 1995. The letters refer to the appended sketch-plan. The mine plan (figure 18) will also be useful.

My first visit was in April in a full wet suit, straight into chest-deep water and three flat-out crawls, leading to a narrow stope up to daylight (A). There is then waist-deep water and an area of stopes, about 15 foot high with much timberwork (B), followed by a bait area (C).

The adit trends ENE with many twists and turns on the lode. Two blocked passages (D) on the right may have connected with Wemyss mine. After about 400 metres, a large chamber (E) about 50 feet high is reached. Also in this vicinity, the shot-holes change direction, denoting two-way driving and very accurate dialling. (Note: These workings are on a north lode which outcrops about 20 fathoms north of Boundary Shaft. It was presumably here, about 1848, that the Frongoch 24 fathom level driving west, holed through into the Wemyss adit. (See page 23 - D.E.B.)

The level continues about 60 or 70 metres to a forehead. Some 20 metres before this is a cross-cut south to Boundary Shaft (F). The adit has a timber catwalk, which proved useful later. The shaft is blocked at roof level and below by rusty metal. Nearby is an iron kibble and a long hooked bar for pulling it in from the shaft. Going east takes you under a stull to a forehead(G), but, a climb up a short ladder leads on. At one point the adit turns north and goes through a heavily timbered area stoped above and below (H). After a flooded winze, the solidly filled Williams' Shaft is reached. The adit circumvents it as before, no doubt to keep adit water out of the shaft.

About 20 metres further on, the adit was blocked by a collapse (I) which had left a cavity above. There were signs that attempts had been made to get through, and therefore I returned on May 14th with a long iron-bar and digging equipment. By probing on the left to avoid the previous efforts to dig straight ahead, I was able to generate a draught. After this, I was through in a couple of hours. After some 20 metres, the adit beyond reached a Y junction. The right branch went into a large stope (J) with a wooden launder in the floor. There was a mass of clog prints, some as small as children's. The level continued through the stope to a collapse.

PLATE XVIII. A view up Engine Shaft from adit level, showing two massive timber pump-rods and a collapsed iron rod on the left. A fourth rod, also timber, is obscured. (R.A. Southwick).

PLATE XIX. Cara Allison examines a wooden wheelbarrow in the adit near Engine Shaft. (R.A. Southwick).

The left branch went on some 80 metres to Engine Shaft, which is open beyond the range of a cap lamp - no doubt almost to surface. At floor level, however, it is blocked with debris. The pump rods, rising main and all sorts of bits and pieces are all in situ, including a wheelbarrow in a nearby level, making a most impressive sight. Just beyond the shaft, the adit is blocked by a fall on the vein, and further progress appears impossible. There is evidence that in wet weather the shaft area is under several feet of water.

On returning to Boundary Shaft and going west, the adit passes a blind heading on the left and comes to a flooded stope (K) where water is rising and there is a short ladder up to what was once a timber platform (Plate V). There is a rise here to higher workings.

The stope was crossed with an inflatable buoyancy aid. Beyond, through waist-deep water, another flooded stope was reached. It would have been very difficult to climb out of the water at the end, but for a ledge on the left. I now found myself standing on a bridge of rock a mere foot wide. In front, a winze about two metres across had sheer sides about 1½ metres down to water (L).

Returning to the adit, I removed a section of the heavy timber catwalk to act as a bridge. I had fitted traverse lines across the stopes for future safety and convenience, without which, getting the timber to the winze would have been impossible. Further west, another flooded stope about 15 metres long was reached, with a catwalk for about half its length. Beyond this were many old clog and boot prints. After about 40 metres, the level came to an end, with another flooded winze (M) descending to unknown depths. (Note: This point would correspond to the Frongoch-Wemyss boundary. From the mine plan, see Fig.18, it is very interesting to observe another 24 fathom level south of the main adit, and presumably on a south lode. This level appears to have been driven into the Wemyss mine, and was linked to the main adit by a cross-cut from William's Shaft, if not elsewhere. - D.E.B).

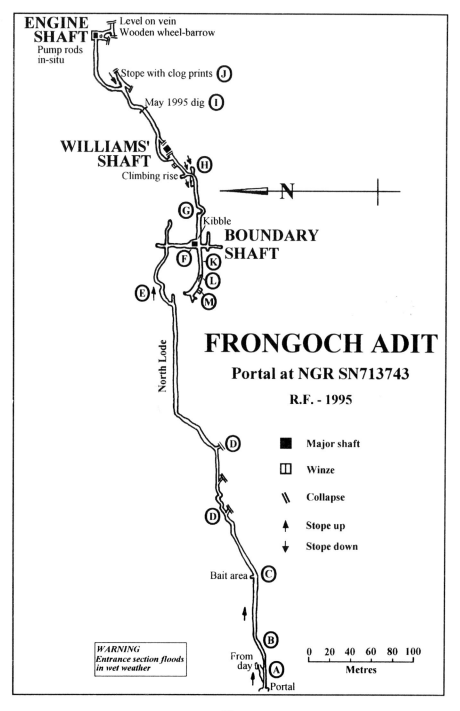

ENGINE SHAFT
Level on vein
Wooden wheel-barrow
Pump rods in-situ

Stope with clog prints Ⓙ

May 1995 dig Ⓘ

WILLIAMS' SHAFT
Climbing rise

Ⓗ

N

Ⓖ
Kibble

BOUNDARY SHAFT

Ⓕ Ⓚ
Ⓛ
Ⓔ Ⓜ

North Lode

FRONGOCH ADIT

Portal at NGR SN713743

R.F. - 1995

Ⓓ

■ Major shaft

⊞ Winze

\\ Collapse

↑ Stope up

↓ Stope down

Ⓓ

Bait area Ⓒ

↑

Ⓑ

WARNING
Entrance section floods
in wet weather

From day

Ⓐ
Portal

| 0 | 20 | 40 | 60 | 80 | 100 |

Metres